Celtic Mythology

Delve Into The Depths Of Ancient Celtic Folklore, The Myths, Legends & Tales of The Gods, Goddesses, Warriors, Maidens, Monsters & Magic

Sofia Visconti

A SPIRITUAL START!

Start your week with gratitude, joy, inspiration, and love.

Healing, motivation, inspiration, challenge and guidance straight to your inbox every week!

FIND OUT MORE

Table of Contents

Introduction

Since we were small children, we've learned of fairy stories, tales of great heroes, Gods, Goddesses, and mythical creatures such as unicorns or dragons. They capture the imagination, teach various life lessons, give hope, and encourage you, especially for most children who grow up in Brittany, Scotland, Cornwall, Wales, and Ireland. Children lucky enough to grow up in these societies get to live the tales as they passed from generation to generation. Some schools still teach mythology in these areas to keep the old traditions, beliefs, and ways alive.

To the rest of the world, however, mythology and related subjects can be quite confusing. Instead of getting lost in the romance, power, intrigue, and magic of mythology, you might often end up getting frustrated with the complexity of the way the story is written. I have published many books about runes, astrology, tarot, the Wiccan ways, and ancient mythology. My books are popular because they are well structured, engaging, entertaining, and written to take the reader on a journey through the topic.

Celtic Mythology: Delve Into The Depths Of Ancient Celtic Folklore, The Myths, Legends & Tales of The Gods, Goddesses, Warriors, Maidens, Monsters & Magic delves into the depth of Celtic mythology. By the end of this book, you will know who the Celts were, as well as their beliefs; you will also have a better knowledge of their Gods and Goddesses. If you were looking for a book about Celtic mythology to captivate your interest, this book is for you. You will learn about heroic adventures, mythical creatures, intriguing fairy tales, fair maidens, magic, folklore, and more.

Who Were the Celts?

The Celts were an extensive collection of tribes that originated in the central European Alps. They were a group of people from all walks of life, such as nobility, farmers, druids, commoners, noble knights, and warriors. The Celtic culture has been around since 1200 B.C. They were a nation that grew to occupy most of the European continent, expanding from Turkey in the east through to Ireland in the west. The Celts were the power in central Europe for many years before the Romans.

The Celtic people were bound by their customs, beliefs, and language; each tribe acted independently of the other. They had no formal governance or organization, although they valued their nobility, serving them with honor and pride. The Celts took war seriously and put a high emphasis on winning their battles. They also honored their Gods and Goddesses with significant monuments and festivals, which they celebrated through their astronomical calendar.

The Celtics would honor their dead by constructing tombs aligned with the stars. All of nature and her creatures were viewed as sacred to the Celts and treated with great respect. Celtic mythology has been around for as long as the Celtic people have, but it was never well documented except for bits and pieces put together by the earlier monks. It was the Romans that first recorded the Celtic beliefs, but they saw the Celts as barbarians and their enemies. Thus, many of the Roman accounts of the Celtic way of life were tainted. The Romans recorded the Celtic God's names with the Roman equivalent for them. It was mostly Christian missionaries in the eleventh century that transcribed the various pieces of scripts that had been written by the druids on bark or wands of aspen. The Celts were highly intelligent and excellent artisans and engineers; they wrote in a script called Ogham. But to them, their culture was of the utmost importance, and they preferred to pass down their stories, beliefs, knowledge, and skills verbally.

As you can imagine through the ages as stories passed from generation to generation, elements were added to them or exaggerated. Some stories were probably lost altogether, either forgotten or woven into another tale, leaving us with the ones we have today. Most of the myths, legends, and stories about Celtic mythology, as we know it in the modern world, come from the Welsh and the Irish. Legends that originated in Brittany, France, such as Isolde and Tristram, were retold by the Irish or Welsh. When the Romans started to be the dominating force in Europe, there were not many Celtic regions except for Britany, Spain, Scotland, Ireland, Cornwall, and Wales. Today the most abundant remaining Celtic culture can be found in Ireland, Scotland, and Wales.

Celtic Beliefs

The Celts had hundreds of tales, which would be sung in a lyrical form by the bards or by stories the village elders would tell. Each tribe of Celts had their own Gods that they worshiped to keep their village safe and prosperous. There are, however, a lot of commonalities between their Gods, stories, myths, creatures, and legends. Most of the Celtic mythology, as it is known today comes from the Irish.

Celtic Mythology has two main groups; each group shares a related language and beliefs. These groups are called Brythonic, for Cornish, Brittany, and Welsh, and Goidelic, for Irish, Scottish, and Manx.

Celtics Ways of Worship and Religious Sacrifice

The earliest Celts built significant monuments in their Gods' and Goddesses' honor, but Nemetons were the place they would gather or go to worship them. A nemeton is a large grove of trees which the Celts held as sacred. References to how sacred trees were to the Celts are in the tales of heroes or heroines named after trees.

The custom of building temples of worship came about during Roman times for the Celts. This was a tradition that they passed on to the tribes that displaced them, such as the Germanic tribes. The Romans like to paint the Celts as a bloody barbaric race that would participate in human sacrificial rituals as a standard practice.

Julius Caesar himself wrote, "In times of danger, the Celts believed that unless the life of a man is offered, the mind of the immortal gods will not favor them" (*Classic Authors Writing About the Ancient Celts*, n.d.). Up until quite recently, it was thought that a lot of what Julius Caesar and the Romans had written about the Celtic beliefs was hearsay. Archeologists have found that the Celtic druids may have practiced human sacrifice and maybe even cannibalism (Owen, 2009).

In ancient times tribes would go to any lengths to win if that meant taking the potions mixed by the druids or sacrificing prisoners or even their noblemen. As stated before, the Celts held victory in the highest regard and thus had some of the fiercest warriors.

Some of the Druids, such as the Druids of Erin, were considered to be sorcerers; they told fortunes, prophesied, made charms, and put a lot of faith in luck. Thus, they believed there were lucky and unlucky days and would look out for omens. As they mainly worshipped the sun and the moon, many of their festivals and rituals revolved around certain days of the year, such as November for Samhain (moon) and May for Bel-Taine (sun).

Chapter 1: Deities of the Celts

There are many different Gods and Goddesses throughout Celtic mythology, but there are a few common deities or variants of some of the more popular ones.

Popular Celtic Gods and Goddesses

The following deities are the more well known of the God and Goddesses in Celtic mythology. Some of the Celtics groups may have a different name or a variant of their name. As scholars of modern times that study Celtic mythology come to find, the Celts were not very good at keeping their pantheons in a neat row—contributing to the reason why one may see different versions of names of one deity.

The All-Powerful God

The Dagda (translates as the Good God), was the supreme God of the Celts. The Dagda is referred to as Sucellos in Gaul, where he is depicted with a hammer and cup.

Unlike in most other mythologies, the Supreme Celtic God was not the God of anything in particular, like the Supreme God Zeus in Greek mythology, who was the God of the Sky and Thunder.

In Irish mythology, The Dagda is always referred to as having immense power and holding a club. With one blow, The Dagda's club could kill nine men. The hilt of the club, however, could bring the dead back to life. The Dagda is usually standing near or next to a cauldron that was known as the Undry. This cauldron was one that could fill up everyone in the village and keep their bellies full, as it was a bottomless cauldron.

The Dagda was the protector of the various Celtic tribes. He watched over them like a father-figure and made sure the village was kept safe as well as prosperous. In Ireland, he was the king of the Tuatha de Danann. The Tuatha de Danann were the children of an earth Goddess named Danu. Danu has no surviving tales about her origins other than being the mother of the Tuatha de Danann. There is also a lot of debate about her name and the meaning thereof (*Danu (Irish Goddess). n.d.*).

The Dagda rose to power by defeating Nuada. The laws in those days stated that for a person to become king, they had to be fit and their body whole. The Dagda wounded Nuada and took over his throne as the All-Father. He lived in a place called Brú na Bóinne, a known philanderer that had many lovers and lots of children.

The Dagda was said to be a giant of a man. Because of his size, his clothes were always too tight, and his stomach would stick out of his shirt. The same was true for his trousers, where the top of his buttocks stuck out. He was an offish God that wore a woolen cloak. His face was unshaven, leaving him with a long curly, unruly beard. Because of his incredible good looks, people barely noticed his attire. He may have been offish, philandering, and quite offensive, but he was also witty, wise beyond compare, and Wiley.

The Dagda's holy day is the 9th of August.

The Queen of Demons, or Phantom Queen

The Morrigan, sometimes spelled Morrigna, was the wife of The Dagda. Her name may sound familiar to those who love the Arthurian legends where she was known as Morgan le Fay or Morrigan the fairy. She was a fearsome deity as the Goddess of destiny and death.

As the Goddess of Fate, Morrigan was turned to before a battle offering favor to the heroes of the battlefields, both warriors and Gods alike. She was a triple Goddess comprising three of the most powerful Celtic Goddesses. She would appear on the battlefield as either a raven or crow to relish over the blood spilled. She would carry off the fallen in a conspiracy of ravens.

War and death are what Morrigan reigned over most of all, she was associated with ravens that would always be present somewhere on a battlefield. Before a battle, Morrigan would appear to either the kings and queens or warriors of the side she favored. For a price, she would offer up a prophecy or share their fate. As she could see everything in the future, including the end of the world, her prophecies were never wrong.

There are many stories where Morrigan appears as three Goddesses, there is a bit of inconsistency as the names of the trio. Although most tend to lean towards her sisters, Banba, Fódla, and Ériu, making up the triple Goddess.

Morrigan's title as the Queen of Demons, or Phantom Queen, stems from her link to the dead and the underworld. She was the daughter of a Mother-Goddess, Ernmas. Ernmas was the daughter of the king of the Tuatha Dé Danann, Nuada. Morrigan's father is not known. Along with her sisters mentioned above, there were another two, Macha and Badb.

Morrigan had five brothers, namely, Ollom, Glon, Gnim, Coscar, and Fiacha.

Master of Skills

Lug or Lugh reigned over kings, rulership, justice, and was the God of the kings. While he lived he was the first Tuatha Dé Danann chief Ollam. This was a testament to him being a judge, ruler, and poet. Upon Lug's death, the position of Ollam became ranked in most of the courts in Ireland. He carried a lightning spear that no mortal or God could withstand called the Assal.

Lug was both a trickster and master of all arts as well as a devious warrior who had no qualms stooping to tricks to get his way. Lug was celebrated on Lughnasa, August the 1st, which is the start of the harvest season. The first of the finest fruit and vegetable pickings for the season would be offered to Lug.

Lug's name has a few possible meanings, some of them include "to bind by oath," which would reference his role as a ruler of contracts and oaths. Another possible meaning would be "artful hands," which would reference his mastery of the arts. One other possible meaning would be "light," as he wields the lightning spear. The most popular name for Lug was "of the long arm" about the long spear of light.

Lug also had a mixed culture which made him a unique character in that he was born from a Fomorian mother, Ethliu. His mother's father was the dreaded Fomorian king Balor. His father was Cian of the Tuatha Dé Danann; Lug's paternal grandfather was a healer of the tribe named Cedh.

Lug grew up with foster parents, but who those foster parents were is a matter of great debate amongst scholars. Some of the potential candidates that pop up in scripts are the Queen of the Firbolg, Tailtiu. Another is the God of the smiths Gavida or Manannán, who was the Irish sea god.

There is no mention of siblings, but Lug did have many wives, namely Nás, Buach, and Buí. Some of Lug's more notable children were Cú Chulainn who he had with Deichtine, a mortal woman. Another would be the son born to him by Nás, the daughter of the king of Britain.

Lug was a highly-skilled character that served as the God of justice. His judging was swift, final, and given without mercy. He is also the inventor of entertainment such as fidchell, which was a game much like chess and horse-racing. He loved sports and many that are still played today he was attributed to.

Lug dwelled at Moytura in County Sligo, and he had another residence at Tara in County Meath.

Ruler of Winter

Caillech is the Veiled One, Goddess of the winds and cold, and controller of the winter weather. Still today there are some places in Ireland, Scotland, and the Isle of Man that believe in Caillech. She is known as a Divine hag that controlled not only how long the winter would be, but how grueling it would be. "Caillech" means hag or old woman, so many scholars think that she may have gone by another name.

Some depict her as Biróg, who saved Lug when he was a baby, or she could have been one of Lug's wives, Buí. There are quite a few regions in Scotland and Ireland that are named after her, such as the "Storm Hag" found in Scotland. "The Hag of Beara" in County Cork, Ireland, is another such place.

Cailleach appears in many different forms, depending on the mythology. In the Isle of Man, she is a shapeshifter that likes to take the form of a huge bird. In other areas, she could commit great feats like riding storms and jumping over tall mountains. Her skin was either blue or an eerie, deathly white, and she had red teeth. She liked to adorn herself in garments from which skulls hung.

Most of the tales about Cailleach don't make her out to be good or evil. She had a hammer that helped her to control the weather and shape much of the landscape. When it flooded it was said to be because of the magic well Cailleach controlled, which had overflowed. She could be a wild destructive force that blew through villages on the backs of raging storms. But she was also a lover of all kinds of animals, for which she was known to tend to throughout the icy winter months.

There were two faces to Caillech, an old hag through the winter and a young woman through the spring and summer. In Irish legends, Caillech was only able to regain her youth in the spring for seven periods. After the seventh period, she had to remain as the old crone she was through the winter months.

In Manx and Scotland's legends, Caillech would transform into the Goddess Brigid. Her transformation would take place at the fertility festival of Beltane on the 1st of May. It was a tradition for the Celt to dedicate the last of the harvested grain to her by using it to start the next crop.

Being the Goddess that forged all the landscape, none could rule over it without first getting her approval. Some of the most inaccessible and unforgiving landscapes throughout the Gaelic Celts is dedicated to Caillech.

The only known family of Caillech was Bodach. Bodach was a trickster spirit, well known in Scottish myths. Although she had quite a few children with Bodach, she also had many others with her many other husbands. Through Caillech's summer transformation back to her youth, she would once again become a maiden. Being an immortal, Caillech got to birth her children, their children, and so on, watch them age, and die. She outlived all of her family and is rumored to be an ancestor to nearly every Celtic tribe in Ireland, Scotland, and the Isle of Man.

Keeper of the Cauldron of Inspiration

Ceridwen originates from Welsh mythology and is a great sorceress, or white witch. There are many ways that her name can be spelled, including Cerrydwen or Kerrydwen. She is known as the Goddess of creation, and has a cauldron in which she brews powerful potions. These potions can change her looks, they can bring about beauty in people, as well as imbue them with knowledge. As a Goddess of creation, she is possibly the most powerful of all the witches of sorceresses in Celtic mythology.

Ceridwen has a magical throne from which she can lend her powers to others at her will. From her cauldron, she offers others the gift of awen, which is the power of insight and spiritual strength. Awen is a status used by the Druids, which is covered in another chapter in this book. Ceridwen's story was told long before the rise of Christianity; scholars deduce that she was written as a sorceress rather than a Goddess by Christian monks.

She is a white witch, meaning she only uses her powers for good and to help others, though her cauldron has both the power to imbue gifts and the power to harm. Once a potion from her cauldron is taken, that person can have the potion again. A few drops could do them fatal harm. On occasion she was known to get upset, but according to the myths she never did much harm.

Tacitus the Bald (Tegid Foel), is Ceridwen's husband and they lived at Bala Lake where he was a formidable ruler. They had a beautiful daughter named Creirwy; she was as fair as any maiden could be. Their son, however, was deformed and a bit demented. His name was Morfran Afaggdu, and it was written that his skin was burned. In Arthurian legend, Morfran is one of King Arthur's warriors.

Later in her life, Ceridwen gives birth to another son, Taliesin. Taliesin is often thought to be the origins of Merlin, the powerful wizard in the courts of king Arthur. Taliesin was a bard, but he was also gifted with his mother's powers. There is more about Taliesin in this book in a later chapter, as he was an important bard and advisor to many a king of Britain.

Ceridwen's cauldron of inspiration appears in many Celtic myths, and she shares some commonalities with other sorceresses in Slavic and Greek mythologies.

The Mother Goddess

Danu, an ancient Goddess, who was known as the mother of all the other Celtic Gods. She is also quite the mystery to Celtic mythology scholars, as there is not much written or known about her. Some theories link Danu to the Danube river which suggests she was a river Goddess with connections to the fairy mounds, dolmens, and fairies themselves.

Royalty would be blessed by Danu with wealth, power, and many other gifts. Danu was the Goddess who ensured that the Tuatha Dé Danann were highly skilled craftsmen and bore many exceptional talents. Even though most of her origins remain a mystery, the Irish depended on Danu to bless everything from good weather to health, and prosperity.

There is no reference to who Danu's husband was, but she was the mother or maternal grandparent to all of Tuatha Dé Danann's divine members.

God of the Wild Hunt

Herne was known as the God of the wild hunt and vegetation as well as the God of the commoners. Like a lot of the Celtic Gods, most of the story of Herne was lost due to poor transcription. He also mainly appears in British Celtic Folklore as he was known to haunt the forests of Windsor. In folklore, Herne was thought to have taken his own life; it was due to the shame of his death that he became a cruel, embittered figure.

He was a ghostly figure that would haunt the Herne Oak tree. People would know he was around when they heard the rattling of chains and eerie moans. All decay that was found in a forest or animal was associated with him. It was said that he could make a tree or creature wither and die by a mere touch. If he came near a farmer's cows he could produce blood instead of milk.

As the stories of Herne progressed he became depicted with antlers upon his head, he carried a horn and was accompanied by vicious hounds. A sighting of Herne was taken as a bad omen that would mean sure death or a disaster would ensue.

Wild God of the Forest

Cernunnos was a horned God that could tame any wild beast or creature. He was known as the mediator of both man and nature. An ancient God of the Gauls with a name meaning "horned one," he was also known as "God of the wild places."

Although he was primarily a God of the Gauls, there are many other Gods throughout Celtic myths that share his likeness and attributes. Some believe that Cernunnos was also a fertility God or God of life because of his love for, and way with, all-natural life.

He loved animals and would have gatherings in the woods where he would feast on wild berries, vegetables, and fruits. The animals that would gather together around him, and did so without preying on each other. Thus wolves, birds, snakes, deer, and so on would all come together in peace around him. Cernunnos could calm all creatures and make them live in peace side by side.

For the rural tribes, Cernunnos was the God that provided for their settlements and protected them against evil or raiders. Cernunnos was depicted with horns and a beard as the spirit of the wild hunt. Thus villagers looked to him for guidance to make their hunting prosperous.

Hearth Goddess of Ireland

Brighid, or Brigid, is the Goddess of life and fertility, she was also known as the Exalted One. Due to her association with life and fertility, she was also the Goddess of spring. She is celebrated on the holiday called Imbolc, which takes place on the 1st of February, mid-winter.

She is primarily an Irish Celtic Goddess, but as with the many other Celtic Goddesses she shares commonalities with other Celtic Goddesses. St. Brigid of Kildare, a Catholic saint, has a lot of similarities to this Irish Goddess. There are a lot of Irish waterways that are named for her and as such, she came to be the Goddess of the Wells.

As the Goddess of life, she was filled with all the contradictions that go with life. On one hand, she was kind, caring, gentle and healing, a nurturing mother figure. On the other side of her personality was a burning fire of passions that would rage against injustice. Her fire and passion were depicted in her image of flowing red locks and her cloak made of sunbeams.

Brighid was an inspirational Goddess which can be seen in the many poems, songs, and text written about her through the ages. Because of her affiliation with the sun, she was sometimes referred to as the Goddess of the sun. Most of the pictures of her show her wearing her cloak of sunbeams referenced earlier in this section. The Celts accredited her with always knowing what was needed, hence her ability to heal and insight. The Imbolc celebrates the breaking of winter's hold over the sun as it starts to return to the land.

Brighid was the daughter of the Dagda, and as such, she had many powerful gifts. Being his daughter lifted her to an exalted position as she was held in high esteem by the Celts. Bres, the High King of the Tuatha Dé Danann, was her husband. They had a son, Ruadán, who was known as the God of mystery or espionage. He was often used by his father to infiltrate their enemies' camps and spy on them to give their warriors an edge on the battlefield.

The God of Storms

Taranis is an important part of Celtic mythology. He is the God of thunder and was depicted by a Celtic symbol of the sacred wheel. Said to move in a flash across the sky, he would travel across the universe at high speed.

The God of storms and bringer of thunder was associated with bad weather. Because of his connection to the sacred Celtic wheel symbol, he was alternatively known as the Wheel God. In our time we at least have a basic understanding of the storms that rip across the skies. In ancient times they did not have the same understanding, so it was only natural the Celtic culture of old would be terrified of them.

It was that terror that drove the early Celts to deem Taranis worthy of whatever sacrifice it took to quiet a raging storm. According to the Romans, if the storm was too great the Celts would have no problem with sacrificing a human to please Taranis. He was the leader of all the other Gods, and as such also their protector. Humans wanted to keep in his good stead, as he wielded a lightning bolt and could move faster than a striking snake.

In Irish mythology, Taranis is known as Tuireann and Ambisagrus in Gaul.

The God of War

Neit died at the Second Battle of Moytura while fighting alongside the Tuatha dé Danann. He was the uncle of Dagda and husband to Badb and Nemain. Neit was the God of War in Irish mythology, a fierce master of the art of battle. The Fomorian Dot was his son and Balor, the king of the Fomorian was his grandson.

There is not a lot written about Neit, though he tends to have played a major role in fighting for the domination of Ireland. In Gaul, he is called Neto and bears a common likeness to Apollo from Roman myths and legends.

Chapter 2: Brittany Celtic Myths

and Legends

Brittany is in the far northwest regions of France, with its capital being Rennes. It consists of beautiful small islands and idyllic coastal towns. Although still spoken in some parts of Brittany, Breton was once the dominant language. It is steeped in Gaulish history and takes pride in its Celtic heritage.

The Bretons were originally from Great Britain. They settled along the shores of north-west Gaul, or what we know today as France. They fled Britain when the Anglo-Saxons invaded and made Gaul their new home, as well as the place where their myths and legends were born. Brittany forms part of the Brythonic Celtic culture.

Popular Myths and Legends of Brittany

Like all the other Celtic tribes, the Bretons held their traditions in high esteem and took their beliefs seriously. This chapter tells the stories of some of the more popular myths and legends of the Bretons.

Ankou

There are not many graveyards in Brittany that do not have a stone statue of a hooded figure guardian at its gates. This stone figure is known as Ankou, a spirit that looks after the graveyard and ensures that the souls of the dead move on as they should. The Ankou is a hooded figure that carries a scythe that bears a resemblance to what we know to be the Grim Reaper. He is often mistaken as death. Often pictures of Ankou will have a wheelbarrow or cart near or with the hooded figure. This is the cart he collects the souls of the dead in.

The Ankou at each gravesite only gets to be the hooded spirit for a year. Each year a new Ankou takes over the role of the watcher of the dead. As legend has it, the last person to be buried at the end of each year takes over the role of Ankou.

The Midnight Washerwoman (Les Lavandières)

There are a few stories about the three women who appear in the dead of night at the water's edge to do the washing. Most accounts of them are of small women with webbed feet and ghostly pale skin. They wash the shrouds of those who are about to die.

These three women are incredibly strong, even though they are quite small in size. They do not like to be disturbed when they are doing their laundry and will curse any who dare do so. They may ask a stranger to help them, and if the stranger refuses they will drown or have a bone in their body broken.

In some stories, the three women are sinners that have been damned for all eternity to wash the shrouds of those about to die. They have been known to wash blood-stained clothes of people who are about to die in battle, and so on. Although they tend to shy away from the living or move them along if they are spotted, they are not to be trifled with. The best way to stay out of their grasp or get cursed is to not be out too late at night.

Mythical City of Ys

Like most myths, there are a few versions of the city of Ys which was fabled to have been engulfed by the sea. The legend has the city of Ys being built by the king of Cornouaille, Gradlon the Great (Gradlon Mawr). Cornouaille is in the Southern part of Brittany. Ys was rumored to be in Douarnenez Bay. It was one of the most beautiful cities around and was built below sea level. To keep the town from flooding, huge sea walls protected the city. When the tide was low the gates of the walls would be left open, but when the seas were high they would be locked tight to keep the water out.

There was only one key to the gate of the tidal walls which Gradlon wore around his neck at all times. Only he could lock or unlock the gates that protected the city. Gradlon fell in love with a beautiful woman who was half human and half fairy. Together they had a daughter, Princess Dahut. Because of his stormy relationship with the fairy he loved, he kept Dahut and raised her in the city of Ys. Dahut loved and worshipped the water and refused to give up her pagan ways, even when her father converted to Christianity.

Dahut was not a nice person and dreamt of only great riches and a place where she could be free to do and live as she wanted to.

To fill the city with wealth, Dahut gifted a dragon to the people who live in the city. The dragon would help them capture merchant ships and fill the city with riches. Soon the city became the richest and most powerful in all of Brittany.

Dahut had a habit of killing her lovers, of which there were many. One day a knight, dressed in red and as handsome as any man she had seen before, arrived in Ys. She seduced the knight and the evening a storm broke out. The knight seemed intrigued by the waves pounded against the walls and gate, but Dahut was not worried. She told the knight that the gates and walls of the city could withstand any storm.

The knight got Dahut to steal the key from around her father's neck while he slept and give it to him. The knight opened the gates in the middle of the raging storm and the waters started to flood the town. It was then that the red knight revealed himself to be the devil and the town, now debauched in sin and fallen into ruin, sank into the sea. Gradlon climbed upon his magic horse, Marvarc'h, but as they started to leave the city, Gradlon was warned to leave the demon Dahut behind. So Gradlon pushed Dahut off his horse and got himself to safety.

Dahut, however, was pulled into the sea and turned into a mermaid (morgen). She became a water spirit that was doomed to swim the sea for eternity. In most myths, mermaids are believed to drown men.

Korrigans

The Korrigans are small fairy-like creatures, with the word Korrigan meaning small dwarf. They are small water sprite creatures that can be found near rivers and springs. Said to appear as beautiful golden-haired lusty maidens during dusk, they lure men into their beds—only their beds are watery graves for any man who is tempted by these small sirens.

If they were to be seen during the day, their appearance would be different and not at all alluring. During the day their eyes are red, the skin all wrinkled, and their hair scraggly and white, much like that of an old chrome. This is the reason why they are not seen during the day, as they hide away so people cannot see what they truly look like.

Much like sirens from dusk and well into the night during the moonlight, they can be seen brushing their long golden hair and singing. Their voice and beauty lure men in, making them fall deeply in love before the Korrigan drowns him.

They were also known to steal human children, especially babies, swapping them out for changelings.

Lady of the Lake

Viviane, or the legendary Lady of the Lake, was believed to have raised Lancelot and stolen the heart of the wizard Merlin. She was the Lady that gave Arthur Excalibur, that proved him to be the true king of Britain.

Viviane was a faerie who enchanted Merlin. Although Merlin could tell his own fate, he could not stop himself from falling in love with her. He built her a magical crystal palace in the waters that surround the Chateau de Comper in Brittany. This palace was a testament to his great love for her.

But Viviane did not return his love, instead, she used him to teach her some magic. Viviane tricked Merlin into meeting her at the fountain of youth, where she restored the magician's youthful features. Once he was young and virile again Viviane trapped him in a magical prison, where he died a slow death.

Merlin

Merlin is one of the most well-known wizards in the world today; even Disney movies have fashioned wizards after him. He was an advisor to Uther Pendragon, and some say he raised Arthur in secret until the day Arthur pulled Excalibur from the stone.

There is not a lot written about the origins of Merlin, but a lot is written about his personality as a joker and his love for wine. He was also a shapeshifter who became a wizard in Arthur's court. It was during his time serving Arthur that Merlin met and became enchanted with Viviane. He was, by then, a lot older than Viviane. She did not return his love; in fact, she was repulsed by him.

Merlin taught Viviane magic and she, in turn, used that magic against him. Paimpont Forest was once known as the legendary Broceliande and is where Viviane trapped Merlin after giving him back his youth at the fountain of youth. Legend has it that Merlin's tomb is somewhere in the heart of the forest, quite close to the fountain of youth.

The Golden Tree

Everyone who knows about king Arthur will know who the legendary Morgan Le Fay is. She is sometimes shown as an evil vindictive sorceress, and other times as she came across as a strong woman. Men feared her with good cause, as she was said to trap and imprison her lovers in the Broceliande Forest—specifically in a golden Chestnut tree that stood in the center of the forest.

She was known as a shape-shifter that would go to any lengths for power and control. She is also a half-sister to King Arthur. In some stories, she takes Excalibur and gives it to Accolon, one of her many lovers. He takes the sword to use it against Arthur but his plot fails. Not wanting to admit defeat, Margan throws Excalibur's scabbard into the lake. The scabbard was what protected Arthur from harm.

Morbihan

The Gulf of Morbihan is said to have been formed from the tears shed by the fairies as they were driven from their home in the forest of Brocéliande. The Gulf of Morbihan lies just south of Brittany, where 368 islands can be found. These islands were believed to have formed from the pretty garlands the fairies either lost or threw in the sea. Houat and Hoedic Islands in the Atlantic Ocean were formed when two of the garlands landed there. The Isle of Beauty in the Atlantic Ocean was formed from the crown of the Fairy Queen.

Megaliths

If you have ever read an Asterix and Obelix book, you would see that Oblix always seemed to be holding a huge boulder in his hands. In Brittany, there are many, many rock formations or standing boulders that have some connection to their myths and legends. Most of these rocks or stone formation can be associated with wizards, druids, and fairies. Some even have more sinister folklore connections.

There are different types of stones such as:

Menhirs

Menhirs are tall stones that are mostly shaped like tall round columns. There are many stories associated with such as worship for the druids and celebrations for the fairies. Because of the shape, they can resemble a human form. This brings about the story of two blasphemous priests that were turned into menhirs in Locarn.

Dolmens

Dolmens looked like large tombs that were made as a burial ground mark. They may also have been used as places of worship. Dolmens were built with four tall supporting stones on top of which was a large flattish capstone. They were all made to stand at an angle with the capstone tilting off to one side.

There is a lot of superstition surrounding these portal tombs, some of which say they were made with the help of or by the fairies.

Carnac Alignment Stones

The Carnac stones are large stones that were positioned across an axis each at a certain distance apart. These stones were mined from local granite by the people of Brittany, who erected over three-thousand of them.

There is a myth from Christian times that the stones are Pagan soldiers that were chasing down Pope Cornelius, who turned them into stone.

Much like the alignment stones at Stonehenge, these were thought to be in alignment with the direction of the sunsets. Some alignment stones were used to mark tombs or druid burial sites.

Steles

Stele were large monumental stones that would often have carvings on them. They were created to commemorate the fallen, as a monument to Celtic gods, or places of magic. For instance, a stele in Seven-Léhart was where sterile women would go on certain nights to rub their bellies on the stone's flat surface. It was believed to be a fertility stone that would allow the women to conceive and have a baby nine months later.

Tumuls

Tumula were dolmens that were not as high as most dolmens, and they were covered with earth. They were mainly used as tombs to house the bodies of the high born.

Chapter 3: Cornish Myths and Legends

Cornwall is one of the six Celtic nations and forms part of the Brythonic Celtic culture. Its history is different from that of the rest of England. Up until around the 16th century, Cornwall was closely linked to Ireland, Wales, and Brittany. During the Iron-Age the Cornovii and Dumnonii Celtic tribes inhabited what is known as Cornwall today.

During the Anglo-Saxon invasion, the Celtic tribes were known as Westwals in reference to West Welsh because of the Celtic heritage. The Cornish Celts stood steadfast in protecting their Celtic heritage and were often at war with the Anglo-Saxons. The River Tamar became a formal boundary between the Cornish Celts and the Anglo-Saxons. The Celts in this region of Cornwall never let go of the culture, even when there was no longer a boundary dividing the two nations. The Anglo-Saxons saw the Celtic nations as fiercely private people who kept to their own kind and closely guarded their customs.

Popular Cornish Myths and Legends

Like all the other Celtic nations, Cornwall's history is steeped in the dark mysteries, intrigues, and romance of myths and legends. This chapter looks at a few of the more popular myths, legends, and stories of the Cornwealas.

Tristram and Iseult

The tale of Tristram and Iseult, or Tristan and Isolde, is one of the most famous of the Cornish legends, as well as the most tragic. It is a tale of deep love, betrayal, and jealousy that ends in the death of the hero and heroine. It is a story about Tristram, the nephew of King Mark of Cornwall, and Iseult, who was the daughter of the king of Ireland.

Tristram's tale begins with tragedy, in that his father was killed in battle as his mother gave birth to him. While Tristram was born as a healthy baby boy, his mother did not recover. To protect the boy from his father's enemies, Tristram was spirited away by his father's trusted companion, Rual, who adopted him. Rual and his wife raised Tristram as their own and taught him in the manner that all royals were. He learned all the airs, graces, and skills that befit a prince.

Tristram was a fast learner and mastered many skills including swordsmanship, hunting, and music. He could play the harp as beautifully as the angels themselves. When Tristram was fourteen years old he was kidnapped by Norwegian merchants. But as luck would have it a terrible storm befell the Norwegian ship. As a superstitious culture, the Norwegian's were sure their ship was being pummelled because they had kidnapped Tristram.

The Norwegian merchants vowed that if the storm subsided and spared them as well as their ship they would set Tristram free. The storm died down and they set Tristram free at the next port, which happened to be Cornwall. From there Tristram made his way into the court of King Mark before the two knew they were related. King Mark was impressed by young Tristram's skills and valor. King Mark made Tristram his confidant, courtier, and companion.

While Tristram was setting himself up in the king's court, poor Rual was searching for his adopted son. He hunted down the Norwegian ship that had taken Tristram and was told that he had been set ashore in Cornwall. Rual made his way to Cornwall where he found Tristram, who instantly recognized Rual. Rual was brought in front of king Mark where he explained who Tristram was. king Mark was both amazed and happy to find out his nephew lived and proclaimed Tristram to be his heir. He also swore to protect Tristram's claim to the throne by never marrying. Tristram was soon thereafter knighted.

King Gurmun and his Queen Iseult (or Isolde) of Ireland used the giant Morold, the Queen's brother, to extract a tribute from both England and Cornwall. Each year the tribute to Ireland would grow and because it was Morold who would come to collect king Gurmun's due, none would challenge the giant. Morold's strength was legendary as was his skill with the sword.

Tristram, however, was tired of his country being oppressed by Ireland and having the threat of Morold hung over them. So he set out to challenge the giant to a duel on a small island in sight of Cornwall. Tristram and Morold each arrived on the small island in their own boats. Morold arrived first and soon thereafter Tristram arrived only to push his own boat back out into the sea.

When the giant asked Tristram why he had done that, Tristram replied that only one of them would be getting off the island alive. As it would be Tristram, he found the giant's boat more than adequate to take himself home.

Morold was fierce and skilled but he was also devious, for his blade was laced with poison. As the furious fight between Morold and Tristram ensued, Morold managed to stab Tristram in the leg drawing first blood. The giant gloated of what he had done to Tristram. He told Tristram that only Queen Iseult knew how to cure the poison that now ran through Tristram's veins. He tried to get Tristram to give up and accept defeat by offering to take Tristram to his sister, the Queen, to be cured. But Morold would only take him if he vowed to continue paying tribute to the king of Ireland.

Instead of relenting, Tristram charged the great giant and knocked him down. As Morold tried to get back up, Tristram managed to cut off the giant's arms with one blow. As the giant screamed out in pain, Tristram brought down another heavy blow that split Morold's skull. The blow to Morlod's head was so intense that a chip of the blade got wedged in the giant's head.

As Morold lay dying, Tristam leaned over his body and told the giant that he now needed his sister's to doctor him because he was the one now seriously wounded. Tristram raised his sword one more time and cut off Morold's head. Ignoring his own wounded leg, Tristram returned to the mainland of Cornwall where he was greeted with cheers for his victory.

Tristram was soon to find out that the giant had spoken the truth about the poison. The wound on Tristram's leg was not healing, but getting worse. He had to make a plan to get to the Queen Iseult. Tristram gathered up his most trustworthy men and set sail for Dublin. When they arrived near the shoreline, Tristram was put into a small boat with his harp and a few supplies.

Although Tristram's wound was dire, he was still able to play sweet tunes on his harp. As the small boat drifted onto the shore some passersby heard his music and went to investigate. They found Tristram and he told the strangers his ship had been set upon by pirates who had wounded him and set him adrift. Tristram managed to charm the strangers into taking him for an audience before the Queen to ask for help. He claimed that he had heard about the Queen's unparalleled healing skills from stories told of her.

When he met the Queen she was impressed with the stories the strangers had told her about his ability with the harp, even while being near death. She took pity on Tristram, thinking him to be a minstrel, and she agreed to help heal his wound. In return, however, she wanted him to teach her daughter, Princess Iseult (named after her mother), how to play the harp.

Tristram agreed to this deal. He told the Queen his name was Tantris and the Queen set about curing Tristram's poisoned wound. It was not long before the wound started to heal enough for Tristram to begin giving Princess Iseult harp lessons.

Tristram was immediately struck at Princess Iseult's beauty, of which he thought none other was near equal to. The Princess was not only a fair beauty but a keen and eager pupil who became nearly as adept at playing the harp as Tristram was under his tutelage. Trist was so taken with her magical voice that he compared it to that of a siren's voice that could tempt and lure a man to give up their heart.

Once Tristram was fully recovered from his leg wound and the princess well versed in playing the harp, Tristram knew he needed to leave Ireland. He also knew that the Queen would not let him leave without just cause. Knowing how sacred the Queen held holy wedlock, Tristram told the Queen that he had to leave because he was married and had a family back in Cornwall. He knew that the Queen would bid him his leave if he told her that his wife had to be his first loyalty. So the Queen bid him his leave to return to his country of Cornwall and to a wife he did not have.

King Mark was overjoyed when his nephew returned, fully recovered from the giant's near-fatal wound inflicted upon him. However, the king's followers were not happy with the fact that he had vowed not to wed and less happy that the king protected Tristram so fiercely. They did everything they could to make Tristram look bad or unworthy in the king's eyes, but nothing worked. The king remained true and loyal to his only nephew.

In his recounting of how he had tricked the Queen into healing him, Tristram had told King Mark of the princess. He had sung her praises and painted a picture of her unrivaled beauty to king Mark. Upon hearing of this, King Mark decided that Princess Iseult was to be his bride and no other would do. The princess would also ally Ireland to Cornwall, and Cornwall could use such a powerful country to back it up.

The problem was that Cornwall and Ireland were sworn enemies. There was no way the king of Ireland was going to let King Mark bid for his daughter's hand in marriage, and King Mark had no way of wooing the princess of Ireland.

Tristram thought up a cunning plan to help his uncle win the hand of Princess Iseult. Tristram had heard about a dragon that was plaguing the lands of Ireland. The word was that the king was so upset about this beast that he had offered the hand of his daughter to whoever could slay the wretched beast. Tristram offered to be his uncle's spokesperson to Ireland and king Mark agreed to Tristram's plan.

Tristram once again set sail for Ireland, and once there he hunted down the voracious fire-breathing beast until he found it. Armed with a shield, sword, and spear, Tristram attacked. It was by no means an easy battle, as the dragon was large, had sharp teeth, claws, and could breathe fire. But Tristram did not back down and stood his ground, finally defeating the beast. Tristram was exhausted and bore wounds from the attack of the dragon, but he knew he would have to get proof that he had slain the beast for the king.

Using the last vestiges of his strength, Tristam managed to pry open the great jaws of the dragon and cut out its tongue. He put the tongue in his pocket not realizing that it was a poison that would seep into his system. Exhausted, and sick from the poison, Tristram dropped himself into a shallow pool to keep himself alive.

At the court of the king of Ireland, another suitor was vying for Princess Iseult's hand. The king's chief steward wanted her badly, despite his ardor not being reciprocated. This steward happened to stumble upon the slain dragon, and having heard nothing of anyone claiming the kill, he claimed it for himself. This devious steward made sure friends and others witnessed him with the dragon. The steward cut off the dragon's head and took it to the king. Here the steward lay claim to the hand of the Princess for slaying the beast that was terrorizing the land.

This did not make the Princess Iseult happy, so she shared her grief and anguish with her mother. The Queen was a woman adept in a certain magic, and she had an inkling that what the steward claimed was not true. The Queen had a vision, and in that vision, she pictured a handsome man that had slain the dragon. She also saw that the man was wounded and had fallen into a shallow pond.

Together the Queen and the Princess hurried to where the Queen knew the handsome hero to be. There they found Tristram barely conscious, lying in a shallow pool of water. While the Queen was trying to revive him, she found the dragon's tongue in Tristram's pocket. The Princess recognized Tristram as the minstrel Tantris and told her mother as such.

The Queen asked a now semi-conscious Tristram if he was indeed the minstrel Tantris to which he replied he was. She asked him why he was back in Ireland to which Tristram told her he was seeking safe trade as a merchant from Ireland. That is why he had slain the dragon, in the hopes that the king would grant him favor and protection.

As Tristram had done Ireland a great favor by slaying the awful dragon, the Queen promised Tristram Ireland's protection. She had him taken back to the castle where she once again nursed him back to health. It was during this time that the now more mature Princess Iseult began to notice how handsome and manly Tantris was. While Tristram was recovering, he had heard that another had laid claim to his kill and the claim for the princess's hand. He knew too that the princess was not in favor of the steward laying the claim.

Tristram was nearly fully recovered when the princess found Tristram's sword and recognized the piece missing from it. The nick in the sword matched the mark in her uncle Morold's head. She immediately held the sword defensively at Tristram and got him to admit the truth.

The Queen found them and the Princess explained who Tristram was and that she was going to kill him. But the Queen forbade it, telling the Princess that they had already granted Tristram protection.

Tristram took the opportunity to offer the two ladies a deal. He would solve the princess's problem of disproving the stewards claim to her hand a lie. He would also offer a match for the princess to King Mark of Cornwall. Both the Queen and the

Princess agreed to Tristram's proposal and so the deal was done.

When the the dragon's head was presented to the king by the steward, the steward promptly demanded his reward. This reward was the promise of the the pricesses princess's hand in marriage. Tristram was able to disprove the stewards' claim to killing the dragon as he had the dragon's tongue, proving the dragon had been killed by Tristram and not the steward who had found its lifeless body.

As King Mark had already agreed to the arrangement, it was not that hard for Tristram to get a contract between King Mark and Princess Iseult. Tristram was to escort Princess Iseult back to Cornwall for her marriage to King Mark. The Queen set about making a very potent potion, which she entrusted to the princess's confidant. The potion was to be given to both king Mark and Princess Iseult upon their wedding night. It was a potion that would ensure they had a marriage of blissful love. The potion was mixed with a bottle of wine.

During the voyage from Ireland to Cornwall, Tristram and Iseult did not get along and clashed when their paths crossed. The weather was also not in their favor during the voyage. Storms made the journey very choppy, and as a result nearly everyone on the ship became seasick. To give the crew and passengers a break, Tristram had the ship dock at the next seaport they came across so all those aboard could regain their land legs and well-being.

The only two who stayed aboard the ship were Tristram and Princess Iseult. While alone on the ship they had time to talk about trivial matters. They went to find something to drink and came across the bottle of wine Iseult's mother had given her companion. Thinking it only wine, they drank the contents of the bottle together.

Brangaene, the one who was entrusted with the love potion, then returned to the ship. She immediately recognized the bottle of wine that was being shared between Tristram and Iseult. Brangaene snatched the bottle and threw what was left into the sea warning the two that no good was going to come of this.

Not long after the wine was thrown into the sea did Iseult and Tristram began to realize that they no longer hated each other. Their hate, mistrust, and animosity had been replaced by the exact opposite emotions. They had fallen in love and could not bear to be parted for too long. By the time they returned to King Mark's court Iseult faced another problem, as she could no longer call herself a maiden. To make sure King Mark was not made aware of this, on the wedding night, Brangaene was who the king unknowingly took to his bed. As time passed, Tristram and Iseult's love, as well as their affair, only grew stronger.

King Mark grew more and more suspicious of his wife and nephew as time went on, until one day King Mark was forced to banish both Tristram and Iseult from his court. The two took refuge in the nearby forest and found a cave where they could stay. They were undisturbed for a long time, until one day the king's hunting party found them. But before they could peek in the cave where Tristram and Iseult were, the two hatched a plan. What the huntsmen saw when they looked in the cave was Tristram and Iseult sleeping on the crystal floor with a sword forming a barrier between them. The king took this as their loyalty and fidelity, and welcomed them back into his kingdom.

Thereafter it became harder and harder for Tristram and Iseult to be together so they decided to end their affair. Tristram left Cornwall to make his home elsewhere, before he left Iseult gave him a ring. The ring was a memento of the deep love they shared. Tristram left Cornwall on a ship bound for Normandy with a very heavy heart.

He made Arundel his home, a small island that sat between Brittany and England.

It was here that Tristram met Kaedin and his sister Iseult. Kaedin was a knight and Iseult was lovely and unwed. As Tristram was staying in Kaedin's castle, he and Iseult were often found in each other's company. It was only to be expected that Tristram would find himself thinking about her in a more desirable way. Tristram was confused over what he felt for Iseult, but over time he gave in and married her. On their wedding night, Tristram made up an excuse not to sleep close to his new wife. He told her that he had an old injury that was causing him pain.

Tristram could not bring himself to touch his new wife, and one day Kaedin found out. He confronted Tristram, who told his friend everything. Not long after that Tristram was injured in a battle with a poisoned spear, while in Kaedin's service. Tristram knew that only Queen Iseult, the love of his life, could save him as she now possessed her mother's healing abilities.

Kaedin set sail for England, as this is where Queen Iseult now resided, hoping to get her to agree to come back and help Tristram. Tristram told Kaedin that if she agreed to come back with him, he must fly both a black and white flag. If not, only a black one. He told Kaedin that this would help him know what was to come of him before Kaedin reached land.

What Kaedin and Tristram did not know was that Tristram's wife had overheard the entire conversation. She knew what the plan was, and her jealousy rose into hatred. When the ship returned Tristram asked his wife if she could see the ship's flag, and if so what color were they. Tristram's wife went to look and came back to tell him that the flag was black and only black.

Tristram knew that it was not only his wound that was sealing his fate but his broken heart and spirit. He repeated "Dearest Iseult" four times as his heart broke and he closed his eyes for the last time. But Tristram's wife had lied out of spite and jealousy, as the ship had both black and white flags. Iseult had indeed come to help her love, but upon embarking, they were told that Tristram had died.

Iseult the Fair ran to where Tristram lay dead, she laid her head upon his chest proclaiming that he had given up his life for her and so she would give up hers for him. Those were the last words she spoke, as she, too, died on the spot in her lover's arms.

Tristram and Iseult were buried next to each and a rose vine grew from each of their graves. As the rose bushes grew their branches met and intertwined joining the two lovers forever and proving that love conquers all.

Chapter 4: Welsh Celtic Myths and Legends

Wales occupies the western part of the United Kingdom. It is nestled between the Bristol Channel in the south and England to the east, with the Iris Sea surrounding it on the north and west. Due to the location of Wales, not many invaders conquered Wales, nor did they mix with the inhabitants of that part of the British Isles.

Still today the Welsh maintain their proud Celtic heritage with their own language and culture. The craggy shores and diverse lands of Wales add to the colorful Celtic myths and legends with their renditions and unique stories. The Welsh form part of the Brythonic Celtic culture.

Popular Welsh Myths and Legends

Wales was inhabited by neanderthals, and later homo sapiens, that came to the land over 30,000 years ago. As man developed through the ages, so did their many myths and legends about the world and the beings in it. This chapter looks at a few of the more popular myths, legends, and stories of the Welsh.

Lludd and Llefelys

This is the story of dragons, demons, a thieving wizard, and two kingly brothers. In the early years of Wales and Britain, a wise king named Llefelys ruled France while his brother Lludd ruled Britain. It was ancient times where demons, dragons, and magic prevailed throughout the kingdoms of both Britain and France.

Britain, however, became overrun by a demonic trice that was called the Coraniaid. This was not King Lludd's only problem; the people of Britain were also being terrified by the most awful, mysterious screams. The screams were so bad they were said to make women miscarry and leave animals barren. The screams were also making crops not produce. On top of all these problems plaguing King Lludd's kingdom, provisions kept vanishing from the court.

King Lludd called upon his brother king Llefelys of France for help. King Llefelys helped his brother by telling him about a potion consisting of water and crushed insects. The potion would destroy the Coraniaid. They devised a trap that caught the wizard stealing supplies and made him subservient to king Lludd.

After investigation, it was found that the awful screams were coming from two fighting dragons. King Llefelys told King Ludd that he needed to dig a hole in the middle of Britain. The hole or pit needed to be filled with mead and then covered with a cloth. The two dragons got trapped in the cloth and were buried far underground in North West Wales, at Dinas Emrys.

Dinas Emrys

There is a legend that surrounds Dinas Emrys that also involves two dragons. King Vortigern tried to build a castle on top of Dinas Emrys, but was unsuccessful. The King could not understand why the walls that had been built during the day would be destroyed each night.

King Vortigern sought the help of Myrddin Emrys (Merlin the wizard). Myrddin told the King that there were dragons that were trapped in Dinas Emrys. Each night they would fly around in the mound, fighting.

The king got his men to dig up the mound and release the dragons. There was a white dragon and a red dragon. When they were released they brutally attacked each other and the red dragon killed the white dragon. The red dragon returned to his lair and king Vortigern was able to build his castle upon Dinas Emrys.

The castle was called Dinas Emrys in honor of Myrddin and the red dragon became a celebrated figure in Wales.

The Devil's Bridge

There is a tale of the Devil that visited Wales in the 11th century. He appeared in the form of a human. There he came upon an old woman staring across a river. She seemed very upset and so the Devil approached her asking her what was wrong.

She told the devil that her cow had crossed the river and she had no way to get it back. The Devil saw this as a great opportunity to get a soul, so he made a deal with the old lady.

The Devil promised the old lady that he would build her a bridge, and in return he got to keep the first living thing that crossed the bridge. The old lady made the deal and went home on the promise the bridge would be built for her the next day.

That night, upon reflection, the old lady wondered about the stranger and his offer. Although it was a very tempting one, the old lady thought, if she was the first living thing across the bridge she would not get her cow back.

The next day the old lady set off to the bridge only this time she took her old farm dog with her. When she got to the river, to her surprise was the most beautiful bridge she had ever seen. The Devil saw the old lady and told her that he had lived up to her end of the deal now it was her turn to do so.

The old lady walked to the edge of the bridge, stopped, drew out a piece of bread which she threw onto the other side. The huge dog took off after the bread. The Devil looked on in disbelief and screamed at the old lady that he could not use a dog. The Devil disappeared in a cloud of anger and the old lady was able to cross the bridge to get her cow.

The Devil was never again seen in Wales.

Gelert

Another well-known legend in Wales is the story of a dog named Gelert. In Wales there is a village called Beddgelert, it thought the town was named after this dog as the town was built around his grave.

Gelert was the favored dog of Prince Llywely of Gwynedd. Gelert was a fearless hunting dog and a gift from King John of England. Gelert was also the Prince's loyal companion. One day the Prince and his Princess set off to go hunting and left their baby son with his nurse and one other servant in their hunting lodge.

The nurse and the servant left the baby prince asleep and unguarded in his crib when they went for a walk in the woods.

While out hunting, the Prince noticed that Gelert was missing. Worried about his dog, the Prince turned the hunting party around to go find him. One of the first places the Prince looked at was at the hunting lodge.

As they approached the Prince saw Gelert run out of the lodge. When he dismounted and upon closer look, he found that Gelert was covered in blood. Panicked and afraid the Prince rushed into the lodge. There he found his son's cradle overturned and blood everywhere. There was no sign of his son.

Enraged and grief-stricken, the Prince drew his sword and ran it through Gelert. Gelert whimpered and died as the cries of the Prince's son could be heard. Shocked, the Prince rushed back into the lodge and behind the crib was his son unharmed. That is when the Price saw the large wolf lying dead and bloodied on the floor near the crib.

Gelert had sensed the baby was in trouble and taken off to go and save it. The dog had killed the wolf and saved the young Prince. Stricken with remorse at what he had done to his dog, especially after such a heroic act, Llywelyn never spoke again.

Llywelyn buried Gelert in a meadow nearby, marking the dog's grave with a cairn of stones. For the rest of his life, it was said that Llywelyn was haunted by the dying sounds of his faithful hound.

Cadair Idris

Standing approximately 893 meters high, Cadair is one of Wale's most well-known mountains. It overlooks the Welsh town Dolgellau in Gwynedd, in northwest Wales. Historically it was the county town of Merionethshire that ran along the River Wnion. The mountain stands at the foot of what is known as the southern gate of Snowdonia.

This mountain is said to be the throne of the giant Idris that sat upon it. The mountain has three peaks: Pen y Gadair, which means head of the chair; Cyfrwy, which means the saddle; and Mynydd Moe, which means the bare mountain.

The mountain is said to have been built as Idris' chair so he could sit in it and stare up at the heavens. At the bottom of the mountain is a bottomless lake called Llyn Cau. At the foot of the mountain are three large stones. These stones were said to have been cast there as pieces of grit that Ibris found in his shoe while sitting upon his throne one day.

There are few of these large stones that can be found in some of the villages around the mountain. Each one said to have been thrown there by Idris, well the larger ones, the smaller being put down by his wife.

The Oldest Tree in Wales

One of the oldest trees in the world is a Yew tree that was planted in a small graveyard around 4,000 years ago. This tree can be found in a village in north Wales—Llangernyw, Conwy. This particular Yew tree comes with a frightening legend. To this tree comes a spirit that appears twice a year to announce the names of the parish members that were going to die that year.

Twice a year the parish members gathered together and listened from beneath the east window of the church to the names the spirit would say out loud. These names were said to be the angel's list. The dates upon which this spirit appears each year are October 31st and July 31st.

The spirit is said to live in the Yew tree and the land upon which the church now stands has always been sacred land.

King March Ap Meirchion

King March Ap Meirchion, or king March for short, is a tale about deformity and the lesson to not to judge a book by its cover.

King March was a king that had everything: riches beyond compare, possessions of every kind, and a rich prosperous kingdom. His subjects loved him, as he was a fair, kind, generous, and just king. His people were happy with their lot in life; they worked hard and lived good lives.

Although he had everything and people saw him as a happy king, he was not. For he bore what he thought was a terrible secret: he was born with the ears of a horse. No one, except for his barber, Bifan, and his long passed parents knew his secret. The king grew his hair long to cover his ears and had a special crown made which covered them up.

Bifan was sworn to secrecy with the threat of losing his head if ever the king's secret were to come out. Keeping the secret weighed heavily on Bifan, and for years he kept his word to the king and the secret was never revealed. Through the years the burden of the king's secret felt heavier and heavier to Bifan until he stopped eating, he became depressed, and fell ill.

A wise and experienced physician was sent to tend to Bifan. The physician examined Bifan and asked him many questions. When he was done he told Bifan that the problem was physically but it was some burden or secret that was causing Bifan distress. Bifan told the physician that he did have a secret one he had sworn a sacred oath to keep. If he did not keep this secret he would lose his life. He did not tell the man what the secret was, only that he had one he could not share.

The physician warned Bifan that if he did not tell the secret he would die of depression. After the physician had left Bifan pondered upon his problem and a solution came to him. The next day he set out into the wilds where there was no one around for miles and miles; it was just him and nature. He found a river that was dense with reeds. He sought a dry spot near the banks where he could lay. As he lay with his belly in the sand and his face near the earth, he told his secret to the ground, the river, and the reeds.

When he was done, Bifan started to feel better. The weight had been lifted from his shoulders and he even felt hungry again. He went back to the town where he had a good dinner and after a few days started to recover.

Back at the court of King March, the king wanted to have a huge feast complete with pipers at the Great Hall of Castlemarch. King March summoned the best piper in all of Wales to play at the feast.

The piper was on his way to Castlemarch when he came across some fine reeds growing at the river banks in a wild spot. He thought that they would make sweet music to play at King March's feast, so he cut some of the reeds. The piper was unaware that the spot where he cut the reeds from was the spot where Bifan had confessed the secret he had been keeping.

It was a merry day at Castlemarch; the feast was well underway. When the guests had eaten their fill, the king decided it was time for the piper to play for them. Having made his new pipe, the piper stepped up and started to play. But what he played did not come out of the pipes; instead, the only sound to come out of them was "King March had horse ears!"

The piper was confused and mortified, he tried to play again but again the pipes repeated the sound about King March's ears. The pipes repeated this statement again and again. The guests were shocked and King March was utterly humiliated; he immediately went to cut off the piper's head. But the piper dropped to his knees in front of the king beginning his merch and explaining it was not him. It was a new pipe he had made from these reeds he had cut on the way to the castle.

Realizing that the reeds must have been the same reeds where he had confessed the King's secret, Bifan came forward. He told the king about his illness and what the physician had said to him. Bifan told the king that he did not want to betray him so he had told the earth in the most remote spot he could find. But the reeds had absorbed this secret and it was not the piper's fault.

King March was hurt and enraged, although it was more his humiliation that influenced his actions, and so he drew his sword on Bifan. But as he was about to cut off the barber's head, he turned to his guests; they stared at him, but not with pity. Something inside the king no longer felt hollow, it felt warm and filled. The king dropped his sword and burst out laughing as he pulled off his crown to reveal his ears.

His guests looked upon their king with admiration and cheered him for his courage. The king forgave both the piper and Bifan, assuring them that no harm would come to them. For the first time in his life, the king felt happy and unashamed. The king learned that day that his people loved him for who he was, and that people will judge you on your deeds–not your looks.

This tale has many lessons in it, it shows acceptance, forgiveness, and human weakness. It is a story that encourages people to be themselves and not be ashamed of who you are.

Chapter 5: Irish Celtic Myths and Legends

The word folklore immediately makes Ireland spring to mind: a country that is steeped in rich traditions, mythical creatures, superstitions, and eerily beautiful landscapes with heartbreaking tales. As with all the other Celtic nations, Ireland consisted of many tribes each with their own chieftain overseeing the village. Although each village had its own chieftain and worshipped their own gods, they did all share a common law system: Brehon law.

The Irish form part of the Goidelic Celtic culture. This chapter looks at some of the more popular Irish myths and legends.

Popular Irish Myths and Legends

Irish history has through the ages inspired poets, authors, and songwriters alike with its ancient heritage of sagas, myths, legends, and battles. It is thanks to the Irish that most of the popular Celtic myths and legends we know about today survived the ages.

Dagda's Harp

The Dagda had a golden harp; it was a magical harp that only he could play. The harp would play the music that could tame a beast, incite his men for war, bring joy, sorrow, or cures for what ailed his battle-weary men.

After the Battle of Moytuirné, which fought between the Tuatha de Danann and the Fomorians, the Tuatha returned home victorious. That night they celebrated their defeat of the Fomorians with a huge feast. The soldiers ate their fill from Dagda's bottomless cauldron that the Dagda took out the sword of the Tethra. The Tethra was a great sword in which a spirit lived. The Dagda ordered the spirit inside of the sword to regale his men with the tale of how the sword came to be.

As the men listened intently, they were unaware that some Fomorians had broken into their camp and stoled Dagda's magical harp.

It was not until the soldiers asked Dagda to grace them with the sounds of his magical harp that he found his sweet-tongued harp was missing. He was enraged and worried as the harp not only played magical music but it helped to control the weather. Without the harp, the farmers and hunters would suffer.

The Dagda asked of his men who would go with him to rescue his harp. The taking of the harp was also of great insult to the Dagda. Lugh Longarm and Ogma the Artificer rose and united with Dagda to embark on the mission to rescue the harp.

The Fomorians and the Tuatha de Danann were two very different people. Where the Tuatha were light and fair, the Fomorians were dark. To reach the Fomorians Dagda, Lugh, and Ogma had to travel through nine valleys, nine mountains, and nine rivers. When they came upon the camp of the Fomorians it was dark, dank, and cold. The camp bore witness to the Fomorians' recent defeat, leaving the people with very little food.

At the edge of the camp, the three men saw that many soldiers protected the harp and they needed a plan to get to it. Dagda was not worried; instead, he stretched out his arm and called for his magic harp. Hearing its true master's voice, the harp sprung from where it had been hung on the wall. The harp flew to Dagda, and the men that got in its way were cut down.

Noticing what was happening, the camp sprang into action, but the harp had found its way back to Dagda. The Fomorians started to advance on Dagda, Lugh, and Ogma when Lugh told Dagda he needed to play his harp.

Dagda swept his fingers across the strings of the harp, and a beautiful melody started to play. It was the music of grief that had the Fomorians stop and bow their head as they sobbed. Even the soldiers sobbed, but they drew their mantles so none could see the tears flowing from their eyes.

The music stopped and again the Fomorians started to charge the three men. Dagda once again drew his fingers across the strings of the harp and this time the music of mirth filled the air. The Fomorians fell into fits of laughter, and once again tears rolled down their eyes as their bellies ached from the laughter. The music stopped and once again the soldiers charged the three men.

Once again, Dagda drew his fingers across the strings of the harp, and this time the music was gentle and soothing. It lulled all in the camp into a deep sleep.

Dagda, Lugh, and Ogma rode away back to their home with the harp back where it belonged. The harp was never stolen again or touched by anyone other than Dagda.

Macha the Goddess of Horses and War

Crunden was a farmer who lived in Ulster and tragically lost his wife. She left him to look after three young children. As he had to work during the day, he had no option but to leave his kids to run amok in the house. The house had fallen into disarray and each day his guilt sliced through him about having to raise his children this way.

One day Crunden came home from working in the fields feeling exhausted and dreading the mess he would find. As he stepped into the house, he could not believe he was in the right place. The kids were sitting all quiet, clean, fed, and happy. The house too was the clean and fine smell of cooking met his nostrils.

As he wandered to the kitchen a beautiful woman stood dishing up a plate of food for him. Macha introduced herself to Crunden and told him that she had come to be his wife and help him. Crunden, a kind and good man, could not believe his luck. He settled into married life with Macha. He did, however, realize that she was not from this world but the otherworld. She did not walk like a normal person, but instead she seemed to glide. Macha, he noticed, could run faster than the wind. They settled into married life together and were quite happy, as were Crunden's children.

One day the king received some new horses that were as fast as any their kingdom had ever seen. The king wanted all his people to celebrate his new purchase, and thus threw a feast. Crunden was invited to go, but before he did Macha made him promise not to say a word to anyone about her. Crunden, not waiting to ruin their life together, promised he would not say a word about her.

At the feast, Crunden had a fair share of wine to drink. While all the other men boasted of how beautiful their wives were or what good cooks they were, Crunden kept quiet and said nothing. This continued until the king stood up and boasted at how fast his horses were. No longer able to hold his tongue, Crunden boasted that his wife was so fast she could outrun any horse.

The king was taken aback and highly offended. He immediately sent his men to get Macha. When his men got to Crundens house they found Macha to be very pregnant. They brought her before the king, who insisted that she race against his horses or her husband would lose his life. Macha agreed, but pleaded with the king to wait until after she had given birth. But the king refused. Macha turned to the king's soldiers and implored them to help her. She knew that a lot of them had families and must know the risks of her running a race so far pregnant.

However, not one warrior stood up for her or came to her aid, nor did any of the other guests. They had all been drinking and feasting, and they thought that this would be excellent entertainment. There was something about Macha that made the king hesitant, and he insisted his chariot not be weighed down with unnecessary objects. He wore no armor and made his charioteer step down.

Macha implored the king one last time to reconsider and wait until she had given birth, but he refused. The race began, and Macha of course proved she was as fast as the wind and won the race. At the end of the race she collapsed onto the grass, writhing in pain as her contractions started. She gave birth to twins on the field—but they were stillborn. In her grief and anger, Macha gathered her lifeless children in her arms. She stood staring at the soldiers. She cursed them for not using their strength and courage to stand up for her.

Because they did not defend her, Macha cursed them for nine generations to come. The curse would render every soldier or warrior in the court's strength to fade when they needed it the most. They would feel the pangs of childbirth for nine days and nights. This curse would go through the next generation starting when a boy child was old enough to grow facial hair.

Macha took her dead twins and left the field; she was never heard of or seen again. But her curse remained true and for the next nine generations before each battle, the men would endure the pains of childbirth for nine nights and night days. Thereafter for nine generations the soldiers of the court of king Ulster suffered the pains of childbirth before each battle.

The Headless Horseman — The Dullahan

Dullahans have inspired many a tale and movie in the modern-day. They are terrifying spectacles that race across the countryside on a demon horse with glowing red eyes. One would think a wild black demonic horse would be enough to scare the wits out of a person, but the demonic horse rider has no head upon his shoulders. Instead, it carries its head mounted on its saddle, beneath its arm, or raised high in one of its hands. The Dullahans head looks like it is pasty and rancid, like dough left to rot and sour. Its black eyes rattled around like they were darting all around the sockets. On his face he wears a smile that looks like it has been carved from ear to ear, and his head glows.

It is said that wherever the Dullan stops, there is going to be a death nearby. This creature can see for miles ahead of him, so he can spot one who is dying from wherever he is. People fear to look upon him for he will poke out an eye or hurl blood in their face. The Dullahan thunders over the countryside on his demonic horse using a human spine as a whip.

Each journey the head can only talk once and when it does it is to call out the name of the one that will die. The Dullahan is mostly seen on the nights of Irish feast days. The Dullahan does not seek out souls but rather responds to cries of a dying soul. He is thought to be the ancient god Crom Dubh. He was a god of fertility, and to give life he demanded human sacrifice each year. The human sacrifice was to be beheaded in his honor.

When sacrificial religions in Ireland were done away with, Chrom Dubh was not happy, so he took on physical form to hunt down souls. It is said there is nothing you can do to ward off the Dullahan, as he is the herald of death. But, he has a fear of gold; wearing an object made of gold may scare him off.

Butterflies and The Wooing of Étaín

In Irish legends, butterflies are the souls of the dead making their way to the Otherworld. One of the most beloved stories about this is the Wooing of Étaín. Étaín was the daughter of King Ailill of Ulaid. Étaín is often depicted much like how Snow White is; her skin was as white as snow, her lips a ruby red, her cheeks flushed, and her eyes an unnatural blue.

Étaín caught the eye of the fair-haired Tuatha de Danann warrior, Midir. Midir lived in the mounds of the earth with the fairy race and was first married to Fúamnach. When Midir came upon Étaín he was smitten and had to have her for his second wife. With the help of his step-son, Oengus, Midir was able to get Étaín's father's approval to marry her.

Midir was so taken with Étaín, that Fúamnach was all but forgotten. Fúamnach became embittered and jealous of Étaín, and devised a way to get rid of her. Fúamnach used magic and turned Étaín in a pool of water, then a worm, and then finally a butterfly. Afterward, Étaín found Midir as a butterfly and stayed close to him. Midir was unaware that the butterfly was Étaín, but got a strong attachment to it anyway. He took it wherever he went. Over time, he lost interest in human women and only cared for the butterfly.

Fúamnach became more enraged, and conjured a wind that blew Étaín seven years into the future. However, Étaín landed with Midir's step-son Oengus. Oengus knew that the butterfly was Étaín, so he created a sweet little glass chamber for her and he too carried her with him.

Once again Fúamnach found out that Étaín had returned to her circle, so she conjured yet another wind to blow Étaín even further into the future. Each time Étaín returned, Fúamnach blew her further into the future until Étaín landed in the wine goblet of the Chieftain Etar's wife. His wife drank the wine, unknowingly swallowing Étaín and soon thereafter became pregnant. Étaín was born again with no recollection of her past.

When she grew up, Étaín married the High King of Ireland, Eochaid. Midir found her again and tried to get her to remember her past. He attempted to trick her into his bed, hoping that if she slept with him it would bring back her memories. But, she evaded his tricks numerous times.

Desperate to win her back, Midir approached Eochaid and tried to trick him into giving Étaín back to him. After being given a series of tasks and challenges by Eochaid, who knew Midir was trying to steal his wife, Midir completed them all successfully. Midir demanded a kiss from Étaín as his prize. Ecochaid agreed and Midir embraced Étaín, kissing her with such a passion that it sparked the memories of Étaín's previous life with him.

Étaín allowed Midir to whisk her way, and they retreated to Midir mound while Eochaid, distressed and mourning his wife, spent the rest of his days digging up every fairy mound looking for her.

Chapter 6: Scottish and Isle of Man (Manx) Celtic Myths and Legends

Like Scotland, the shores of the Isle of Man have been raided by various other nations many times throughout history. This island lies in the middle of the Irish Sea and is an equidistant between Scotland, Ireland, England, and Wales. It is also said to be where the Manx cat, a tailless domesticated breed of cat, originated from.

The King of Norway sold his suzerainty to Scotland in 1266. Like the Scottish, the Manx are superstitious and fiercely proud of the heritage. Their culture is filled with folklore, mythology, and the ever-popular ghost stories.

The chapter looks at some of the myths of Scotland and the Isle of Man.

Popular Scottish Myths and Legends

Misty rolling hills, lochs, rugged mountains, and mysterious creatures form the grounds for Scottish myths and legends. This proud nation has many tales that inspired, intrigued, and warned the Celtic people who once lived there. The Scottish form part of the Goidelic Celtic culture.

Stories of the Loch Ness monster, ghosts that wander the hills, and great heroes echo through the beautiful land that makes up

Scotland. This chapter takes a look at some of the more popular myths and legends of Scotland.

Sawney Bean

This story is about one of Scotland's most famous cannibals, Sawney Bean. Born in East Lothian, Sawney moved to Ayrshire where he married and had a home near Ballantrae in Bennane Cave. His home was a mass of tunnels that ran inside solid rock, into which they excavated a few rooms as their family grew. When he and his wife were first wed, he found himself unemployed and having to find another means by which to support his wife.

Sawney took to robbing stagecoaches or lonely travelers traveling along small narrow roads. These types of roads made it easier for Sawney to ambush his prey and rob them. He worried that his victims might identify him, so to keep his crimes from being discovered he murdered his victims. Butchering them to destroy any evidence would allow him to dispose of the bodies, and from there he could feed his family.

Soon the Beans had fourteen children with a lust for human flesh. As the children grew so did the list of missing persons in the area. Although the local authorities looked for the missing, no one thought to check the caves.

The Bean family grew and the children became adept at finding their prey. One night, however, a man and his wife were riding home from a fair when the Bean family attacked them. They managed to get the wife off her horse, but the man fought them back. They were not prepared for the fight that ensued, nor to be discovered as a troop of other people returning from the fair came upon the man fighting off the savages.

It was not long after that that the search for the Bean family began, and they were found in the caves. What the authorities found was beyond horrific. Human body parts had been pickled and hung from hooks, much like a leg of mutton in a butcher shop. There were piles of human bones, clothes, and other evidence for their crimes.

All of the Bean family was arrested and taken to prison in Edinburgh. Their crimes were considered so heinous that the courts thought conventional law did not apply. Thus, the Bean men had their arms and legs cut off and were left to slowly die as they bled out. Meanwhile, the Bean women were burned alive in huge bonfires.

Strike Martin

On the northern outskirts of Dundee, Scotland is Strathmartine. It was named after a brave young man named Martin. The legend tells of a farm called Pitempton, on which lived a humble farmer and his nine daughters. One night he asked his eldest daughter to go down to the well and fetch some water. When his daughter did not return, he sent his next eldest to go look for her sister. His second eldest daughter did not return either, so he kept sending his daughters until they were all gone.

Worried, he himself went looking for them, only to come across their bloodied bodies laid out in a row. Eating off their flesh was a creature resembling a dragon that looked like it was mixed with a serpent. Frightened, the farmer ran off to seek the help of his neighbors. They all banded together and allowed the farmer to lead them to the well where they found the creature still feasting upon its recent kills.

Outnumbered, the creature tried to make its escape, but a young man named Martin struck the beast down with his club. The crowd cheered as the beast fell and died, and Martin became known as Strike-Martin. The spot where he had slain the dragon became known as Strike-Martin as well, and later it was named Strathmartine. Near the village of Bridgefoot, there is a lone stone that stands in a field known as Martin's stone.

The Ghost Piper

Scotland is full of ghosts and ghost stories that make a person's hair stand on end. One such story was the story of the ghost piper of Clanyard Bay. Scotland is notorious for the wailing soulful sound of bagpipes. Scotland is awash with mountains and hillsides that extend as far as the eye can see. Within these hillsides are often a series of caves or mysterious tunnels that network different villages together.

There is said to be a network of tunnels that start at the Cove of Grennan and extend to the craggy cliffs of Clanyard Bay. In times gone by, the locals believed these tunnels to be where the fairies lived, and none dared to disturb them by going in. One young piper, however, decided to find out for himself if the fairies really did live there.

Armed with his bagpipes and his dog, he entered the caves. He blew loudly on his bagpipes as he walked deeper and deeper into the depth of the tunnels. His bagpipes got softer and softer until they could be heard no more. After a lengthy silence, his dog rushed out of the tunnels whimpering. All the dog's hair was gone, and so was the young piper.

It is said that some nights or at certain times of the day you can hear him play his bagpipes. The sound wails from beneath the ground as he plays.

Brownies and Giants

In Scotland there were tiny little people known as Brownies that were like little elves, only they did good deeds for people. It was said that late at night when the people slept those in need would get a visit from the Brownie people. They would come into the house and do what needed to be done. They were shy and would run away before they were discovered by humans. Many tales incorporate these little people; even the Romans believed in small people who helped out, though they called them Lares.

From tiny people to giants, nearly all mythology has something written about giants. Scotland is no exception. One particularly well known legendary giant is Cailleach, a female giant. In the Forest of Mar in Aberdeenshire is a large formation of rocks that looks like a collapsed house. This is said to be the remains of Cailleach's house and the Alisa Craig island was formed by her when a large pebble fell out of the apron she always wore.

Isle of Man (Manx) Celtic Myths and Legends

The Isle of Man is a small island perched between Ireland and Britain in the Irish Sea. Like Wales, the Island was not of any interest to the invaders of Britain at the time the Celts occupied the land. The Vikings invaded the island in the 8th century and brought with them significant change. The Tynwald is the Isle of Man's parliament and has been around for a thousand or so years.

This small island has been around since about 8,000 years BC, and has its myths developed through many significant ages of man. The Isle of Man forms part of the Goidelic Celtic culture.

The Isle of Man was populated for centuries before the Celts came along, during the Iron Age. Through the different periods of the Island's development many dark, mysterious, and entertaining stories were woven to a captive audience that looked to the bards, druids, and Gods for explanations for things we take for granted today. The event of dying crops was most likely something to do with an unhappy God, a child taken early was some demon's doing, and so on.

Ancient accounts of the weather, death, and natural disasters built up a collection of stories that we read today as myths and legends. This chapter looks at a few of the more popular myths, legends, and stories of the Manx.

The Old Caillagh

Caillagh ny Groamagh was known as the sullen or gloomy old woman. She was thought to have been a witch that was cast out Ireland and into the sea where she would be drowned, only she kept herself afloat and landed on the shores of the Isle of Man on the 1st of February, St. Bridget's Day. To dry herself off, she went about gathering up as many sticks as she could find to light a fire.

The following spring was a very wet one, and the entire spring had only bad weather. The legend that followed was that every ditch on the Isle of Man had to be covered with snow on St. Brigid's Day. This was so that the Caillagh could not find sticks to gather up to dry herself with.

If Caillagh found enough sticks and got dry on the 1st of February, spring on the Isle of Man would have bad weather. If Caillagh could not find sticks to gather and remained wet, spring would have nice weather.

Fairy Bridge and Mooinjer Veggey

On the Isle of man, the little people are called Mooinjer Veggey and never referred to as fairies. This is especially true when crossing the fairy bridge on the south-east of the Isle of Man. The bridge lies between Castletown and Douglas.

When crossing the bridge you have to greet the fairies and if you do not bad luck will befall you. You have to say either:

- Moghrey mie Mooinjer Veggey — Good morning Mooinjer Veggey.
- Fastyr mie Mooinjer Veggey — Good afternoon or evening Mooinjer Veggey.
- Laa mie Mooinjer Veggey — Good day Mooinjer Veggey.

Arkan Sonney

The Arkan Sonney are little magical fairies that look like a pig crossed with a hedgehog. To catch an Arkan Sonney is meant to bring good luck and fortune to the one who catches it. It is a little white pig with hedgehog type quills, and those that cross its path will find a silver coin in their pocket.

The Little Shoe

One day, Mr. Coote saw Molly walking along the side of the road. He saw she was not looking very happy on this day. Mr. Coote loved telling stories of the little folk and fairies that roamed the Isles. He had just the story for sweet little Molly to put a smile back on her cheeks.

He called her, and she stopped to greet him. He asked her why she was so blue and she shrugged; she was not too happy on this day. He asked Molly if she had ever heard of the Cluricaune. As he suspected, she had, as her father told her stories of these little people much like the Irish Leprechaun.

Mr. Coote asked Molly if she had ever seen one, to which she replied she had not. She asked Mr. Coote if he had seen one, but he had not either, though, his grandfather had way back when he was a much younger man. His grandfather had suspected there may be Cluricaune living in the barn, as he had heard scuffling and whistling late at night.

One night his grandfather had gone out to the barn to feed the old mare that was ailing. As he got to the door, he heard hammering like the sound a shoemaker makes. His grandfather was curious, and he slowly stepped into the barn. That is when he saw the little man hammering away at a tiny shoe while singing the sweetest song.

His grandfather looked all over the barn to see if he could find the little creature, and found him hidden in the mare's stable between some bales of hay. The little man was whistling and singing so loudly he did not hear Mr. Coote's grandfather sneaking up on him. Before the Cluricaune could react, his grandfather had captured him in his hand.

Mr. Coote's grandfather laughed in glee, as he had captured a Cluricaune. It is said that if you can get a Cluricaune's purse, you will have endless riches. But the Cluricaune was not about to give up his purse. Mr. Coote's grandfather would not set the little creature to go until the Cluricaunned told Mr. Coote's grandfather that he would need to get it back at his house. So like an old fool, his grandfather opened his hand, allowing the Cluricaunne to escape. He was so excited to be getting the little creature's purse that he did not realize it had tricked him.

The Cluricaunne had, however, left behind his little shoe he had been working on. So Mr. Coote's grandfather took the shoe, and that year his farm gave good crops and his cows had an abundance of milk. To the end of his days, Mr. Coote's grandfather was convinced it was because he had kept the little creature's shoe that such good luck had come to them.

Molly asked Mr. Coote if he had seen the shoe, but he said he had not. But his mother had. They had lost it long before Mr. Coote was born. But every night he still leaves a little of food and water out in his grandfather's old barn just in case the little man comes back.

Molly had loved the story and thanked Mr. Coote for the tale. As she skipped off home and neared the barn of their farmhouse, she heard hammering. Slowly Molly walked into the barn, but there was nothing there except a tiny little shoe. Molly smiled as she picked it up. It was beautiful. She thought about the story Mr. Coote had told her, then carefully put the shoe back.

As she went to get her dinner, Molly was no longer feeling blue.

Chapter 7: An Overview of Popular Celtic Fairy Tales

Not only did the Celtic nation have some of the greatest myths and legends, but they were also excellent storytellers. Each story would be one of either inspiration, encouragement, love, strength, forgiveness, or instead be a lesson or warning.

Some of their fairy tales would be entwined with one of their Gods/Goddesses, heroes/heroines, royalty, or beasts. Others would be of normal everyday people that things would happen to.

This chapter takes a look at some of the Celtic fairy stories from the Celtic nations.

Many of the fairy stories of today have been taken from the fairy stories of old Celtic tales. Here are a few popular Celtic fairy tales that you may find you have heard a different version of.

A lot of fairy stories as we know did originate for Celtic folklore such as:

- The Goose Girl
- Frau Holle
- Clever Hans
- The Girl Without Hands
- Goldilocks and the Three Bears
- The Frog King
- The Pied Piper

There are hundreds of old stories to choose from, below are some of the older Celtic fairy tales for you to enjoy. They have been written as the old story, but in a more modern-day English language.

Jack and His Comrade

Jack lived with his widowed mother, and they were very poor. They grew potatoes and would live from meal to meal, waiting on the potatoes to be fit for eating. One summer, however, the potatoes were very scarce. So Jack decided it was time for him to take charge and seek his fortune.

Jack told his mother that he was going to go out and do what he could to find his fortune. As soon as he found it, he would be back to share it with his poor mother. He asked her to bake him a cake and kill his hen. Jack's mother did as he asked and he set off at sunrise the next day.

Jack's mother walked him to the gate and at the gate, she asked him if he would take only half the chicken and half the cake, or take the whole lot and her curse. Jack looked at his mother and laughed that he would never want her curse. Happy with her son's answer, she gave Jack the full cake and all the chicken for his journey.

Jack walked and walked until he could walk no more, as fatigue caught up with him. He saw a farmer's house and thought to ask for a bed in the barn for the night. As he turned onto the road he found an ass that was stuck in the bog that ran alongside the road. The ass had tried to get to the sweet grass on the other side of the bog when he got stuck.

The ass called out to Jack to help him out of the bog or he would surely drown. Jack, always willing to help, found stones which he threw into the bog until the ass was able to climb out.

When the ass was safely on solid ground, he thanked Jack and promised to pay him back for his good deed one day. He then asked Jack where he was going. Jack told the ass (Neddy was his name) that he was on his way to find his fortune.

Neddy asked Jack if he could come along as he too may find some good fortune. Jack was happy for Neddy to come along on the journey, so they headed off to find shelter for the night. As they passed through a small village they saw a dog with a tin tied to his tail and a troop of gossoons (small boys) chasing it with sticks.

The dog saw Jack and Neddy and ran to them for protection. Neddy was mortified at the treatment of the poor dog so he let out the mightiest of roars, scaring the gossoons. As they ran off, the dog thanked Jack and Neddy then asked them where they were headed. Once again Jack told the dog they were going to find their fortune.

The dog asked if he could join Jack and Neddy as he too could do with a change of scene and be rid of the boys chasing him. The dog's name was Coely. The three of them set out to find shelter for the night and came upon an old wall. They sat down below it, Jack pulled out the provisions his mother had made him, and gladly shared it with his friends.

Neddy decided he would prefer the thistles he found on the side of the road while Coely shared with Jack.

While they ate and chatted, a half-starved cat came over to them, his meow was as pitiful as can be. Jack and his new companions felt sorry for the cat and Jack offered it some food.

The cat's name was Tom and he thanked Jack by blessing him with hopes that one day Jack's children never knew a hungry belly.

The cat asked where they were going, so Jack told Tom and asked if he would like to join them. Tom was delighted by their offer, and when their bellies were full and their feet rested the four of them set off. As they walked and the night shadows grew longer, they heard a great crackling coming from the bushes alongside the road.

As they neared the noise a fox jumped out of a ditch; in his mouth was a large black rooster. Neddy once again roared like thunder, scaring the fox. Jack sent Coely after it. The fox, Rynard was his name, dropped the rooster, and ran off into the night. The rooster was a bit battered and bruised, but he thanked Jack and his friends for saving him. The rooster then asked where they were all heading, so Jack told the rooster they were going to seek their fortune. Jack offered for the rooster to join them, which the rooster gladly accepted.

So they set off down the road again as the night grew later there was no farm or barn in sight. As it was summer night Jack decided they could go into the wood and make a camp there in the long grass. So off they went once again to make a camp in the woods.

Jack stretched out in the long grass, Neddy lay next to him, Coely on the other side, the rooster took a tree and Tom cuddled down in Neddy's lap. They had all drifted into a deep sleep when the rooster decided it was time to crow. Neddy got such a fright he yelled at the rooster for disturbing him from his sleep.

The rooster yelled back that it was daybreak and couldn't he see the sun starting to shine?

But it was not the sun, it was candle light that glowed in the distant dark. The five of them set off to go explore. They found a cabin and from inside they could hear the sound of merriment. Being very quiet, they tiptoed to the window to see inside. There was a band of thieves eating, drinking, and bragging about the theft of Lord Dunlavin's gold and silver. They toasted to the porter at the Lord's house that had helped them steal all the gold and silver.

Jack and his friends decided to scare off the robbers so they could return Lord Dunlavin's gold and silver to him. So Neddy put his hooves upon the windowsill, and Coely jumped onto Neddy's back. Tom climbed up on Coely's back, and the rooster on top of Tom's head.

They started to make a big noise of barking, hissing, and roarings, and Jack shouted at the window for the thieves to surrender as they had the house surrounded. The thieves were deeply frightened and ran off into the woods, leaving their weapons, food, and loot behind. Jack and his friends ran into the cabin, closed the shutters, locked the doors, and finished what was left of the robbers' feast.

Later that night the captain of the robbers decided to double back and go check back at the cabin, but when he got inside the cabin was dark. He quietly snuck towards the fire. When he got there the cat flew at him and landed in the captain's face, scratching at him with his sharp claws. The captain screamed and tried to make it to the door, but he stood on the dog's tail while doing so. As a result, the dog bit him on the arm and legs. Swearing, the captain ran for the door only to have the rooster drop down on his head clawing and pecking at him.

The captain dashed out of the cabin and headed straight for the woods, where he told the rest of his band of thieves how he had been brutally attacked. All the thieves decided it was best not to attempt to go back there.

When the morning came, Jack and his friends had a good hearty breakfast. They collected Lord Dunlavin's loot and set it on Neddy's back. The five friends then set off, headed for Lord Dunlavin's castle. When they arrived at Lord Dunlavin's court, they were greeted at the door by the thieving porter.

The porter asked them what they were doing there, to which Jack replied he had business with Lord Dunlavin. The Porter was shirty with him and told him the Lord did not have a place for the likes of them. But the rooster was not having this thief stop them from their quest, so he challenged the porter about the robbery, making the porter's cheeks go red. It was then that the Lord and his daughter made their presence known. They had been listening to the entire time at the window.

The porter tried to discredit the five friends saying he did not open the door to let the six thieves in. To which Jack replied, "How did you know there were six if you did not let them in the door?"

Jack handed the lord the bags of silver and gold they had brought back and asked for nothing more than a bed and food for the five of them. But the Lord was not having any of that. He told Jack and his friend that they would never be poor again, for what they had done was a truly noble deed.

So the rooster, dog, and the ass got a prime spot in the Lord's farmyard, while the cat got a nice warm kitchen. The Lord took Jack under his wing and decked him as any fine gentleman should be. Jack was made the Lord's steward.

Jack went and fetched his mother, settling her into a nice cozy house with everything she could need. Jack and his mother never wanted for anything ever again.

The Three Crowns

Once upon a time, there lived a king who had three daughters. While his youngest was as good as gold, his two eldest were bossy and quarrelsome. Three princes visited the king's castle, all brothers, and the king found that two of the brothers were just as troublesome as his eldest daughters. One of the brothers, however, was just as good and easy as his youngest daughter.

The king, his three daughters, and their suitors all went for a walk around the lake one day. There they met a beggar. The King would not give the beggar anything, neither would the eldest two of the princesses or princes. But the two youngest out of the brothers and sisters gave the beggar food and treated him with kindness.

As they walked further along the lake, they came across one of the most beautiful boats they had ever seen. The four eldest of the brothers and sisters all said they would take a sail in the boat. The two youngest of the siblings both said they would not like to take a sail in the boat. The youngest did not want to get onto the boat, for she feared that the boat was an enchanted one.

The youngest princess's father finally got her to get on the boat. The princesses climbed aboard first. But when the king and princes wanted to follow, a small man no bigger than seven inches tall sprang in front of them. The princes went for their swords, only to find they could not draw them. The tiny man laughed and told the men to say goodbye to their princesses for they would not be seeing them for a while.

As the little man started to sail away, he said to the youngest of the brothers, fear not, for you will see your princess again. The little man also told the youngest man that he and the youngest princess would live a very happy and loving life. The little man left the men with a final word: "Bad people if they were rolling stark naked in gold, would not be rich." With that, he bade the four men good-bye and sailed away with the princesses.

Although the princesses tried to speak they found that they could not; they had no voices. Once the boat was out of sight the princes and king could move again. They rushed after the ship, but it was gone. But there was a well from which hung a rope, the same rope that had tied the boat to the lake's edge.

When they pulled the rope up, there was a basket at the end of it. The eldest prince was the first to climb inside the basket to go find the princesses. After a day, he did not return. The second eldest prince went down the well to find the princesses. Then on the third day, the youngest prince went down the well while their men stood guard of it.

When he got out at the other end, there was a beautiful garden with a castle in the middle. The prince walked into the castle looking from room to room but could not find a single soul. Eventually, he came across the dining room where a feast was laid out. The prince was very hungry, but thought it was rude to eat other food without invitation. The prince made himself comfortable by the fire and waited.

It was not too long when the seven-inch man came into the room with the youngest princess. The prince and princess rushed to each other, and the man asked the prince why he had not eaten; the prince told him he thought it would be rude.

Seven-inches laughed and told him that his brothers had not felt that way. That is when he saw that his two brothers had been turned to marble statues. The man told the young prince that he would have to rescue the other two princesses from the giants they were imprisoned with.

The next day, the prince set about rescuing the other two princesses from the two giants. The man turned the older princes back to flesh and let them all leave together. But before they could go, the man gave each of the princesses a set of three crowns and told them that they had to wear them on their wedding. They had to all be married together, or ill fate would befall them.

The oldest brothers were not very happy with their youngest brother, and were plotting something against him. The youngest princess heard this, turned to her prince, gave him her crowns, and told him to put a stone in the basket if the eldest two made him go last. When the princesses were safely above, the two eldest brothers made the youngest wait to go last.

When the basket came down for the young prince he put a stone in it. As it was pulled to the top the rope was cut, and the basket with the boulder in it came crashing down. The prince was beside himself, but he had nothing more to do than go back to the seven-inch man's castle. There he was treated to the heartiest of meals and finest of wine, as well as given a comfortable bed. After a week had gone by, the young prince was lonely and missing his true love.

To appease him, the seven-inch man gave the young prince a beautiful snuff box. The snuff box would call the man if ever the prince needed him, as it was time for the prince to leave the castle. He pointed the young prince in the direction of walking, and as he did he felt so tired that he bowed his head and did not pay attention to where he walked.

It was not until he heard a hammering that he raised his head and realized he was no longer at the seven-inch man's castle. His attire was not that of prince's any longer, but of a commoner. He walked past a smith's shop, where the smith called to him and asked him if he was any good with a hammer. The young prince said that indeed he was, and went to work with the smith.

The prince and the smith were turning horseshoes when in walked the tailor with news of the royal wedding of the two older princesses. They were all finely dressed with their beautiful crowns upon their heads, but as the grooms walked down the aisle, the floorboard opened and down they fell. The king then decided to put off the wedding until the youngest had her crowns and her groom. The king offered the princess's hand to whoever could make the crowns. The king was also willing to put up the gold, silver, and copper to make the crowns with.

The young prince knew that he could get the crowns down, for he had them hidden beneath his tattered old clock. He sent the smith to go fetch the metal from the king, and promised that he would forge the crowns for him. The smith did as the young prince asked and brought him back the metal.

The prince told the smith to leave and then sealed up the forge tight. That night the villagers heard the hammering and cursing of the young man they thought to be the smith's apprentice. In the morning the young prince handed the smith the crowns. The smith told the young prince to come to the castle with him, but the young prince refused.

When the smith showed the king the crowns he was overjoyed, and offered the smith the young princess's hand in marriage. But the smith could not lie and he told the king it was not he who had made the crowns, but a young man he had taken in the previous day. The king asked his daughter if she would take that young man as her husband but she wanted to see the crowns first.

The young princess recognized her crowns instantly and knew they were from her true love. So the princess agreed to marry the young man who had sent the crowns to the castle. The king told the eldest prince to go and fetch the young man in the king's carriage. They then lived a full and happy life, always together.

Golden-tree and Silver-tree

Once upon a time, there was a great king with a beautiful wife whose name was Silver-tree. They had a daughter whose name was Golden-tree, and she was even more beautiful than her mother.

Silver-tree was a very vain person, as well as a jealous one. She wanted to be the fairest in all the land, so each year she would go down to the glen where there was well with a magic trout. In this one year she went down to the well, called upon the trout, and asked the fish if she was not the beautiful queen in all of the land.

The trout said she was beautiful Golden-tree was more beautiful than her. Enraged, the queen went home and lay down on her bed. She vowed she would not be well again until she had the heart of her daughter Golden-tree. The king was given word that the queen was ill; he went to see what was wrong. The queen told him that she needed the heart of Golden-tree if she would never be well again.

The king loved his wife dearly, but he loved his daughter too, so he sent his daughter away to be wed to a prince in a far off land.

He told one of his huntsmen to find a goat, cut out its heart, and bring it to him. The huntsmen did as he was told, and the king presented the queen with the heart of the goat in the pretense that it was the heart of Golden-tree.

Meanwhile, Golden-tree and the prince were truly in love with each other and started their own happy life far away from her mother, the evil queen.

The following year, Silver-tree once again approached the trout in the magic well and asked if she was not the most beautiful queen there was. Once again, the trout told her that it was the Golden-tree that was the most beautiful queen.

The queen was now even more enraged, having found out that her daughter was still alive and she had been deceived.

The queen then commandeered her husband's boat and took off to the far off land, where her daughter was now wed to the prince. But Golden-tree had gotten word of her mother's arrival, and told her husband of her fears of her mother wanting to murder her.

The prince locked Golden-tree in a tower so her mother would not be able to get to her. Upon the queen's arrival, she called for her daughter but was told she was locked in a tower and could see the queen. The queen found her way to the tower and called her daughter to come and see her mother.

But Golden-tree said that she could not. The queen told Golden-tree to put her finger through the hold in the tower door so she may bestow her daughter with a kiss. Golden-tree thought no harm could come of this, so she did as her mother asked.

Triumphant, the queen pierced Golden-tree's finger with a poison dart, and Golden-tree fell dead to the floor. When the prince found his princess he was devastated, so he placed

Golden-tree in a beautiful glass box in the tower. He locked the door and let no one near it.

Time passed, and one day one of the princess's companions made their way to the tower. There she found her princess laying so pale and lifeless. On closer inspection, the women found there was a poison dart in the princess's finger. The women pulled out the dart, and Golden-tree awoke.

The prince was overjoyed to see his beautiful wife alive and they one again resumed their happy life.

Another year had passed, and Silver-tree once again went to the well to ask the trout if she was the most beautiful queen of all. Once again, the trout responded that Golden-tree was still the most beautiful of all.

The queen was even more outraged than ever, finding out her plan to poison her daughter had failed. The queen set off for the far off land, and this time, she took a bottle of poison wine.

When she arrived, the princess and her companion approached the queen as she came off her ship. The queen feigned joy in seeing her daughter alive and offered her a drink of wine to celebrate. But the princess's companion told the queen that in their land it was custom for the guest to take the first sip.

The queen lifted the glass to her lips, but the companion pushed the glass as she put it to her mouth, and wine went down the queen's throat. The queen gasped as the poison flowed through her, and she dropped dead where she stood.

They buried the evil queen far from the kingdom and celebrated Golden-tree's freedom from her mother, the evil queen.

The Sprightly Tailor

The Laird MacDonald of castle Saddell employed a sprightly tailor to make him a pair of trews. As the tailor set about taking the Laird's measurements, they got to talking about the old ruined, haunted church. It was said that weird things happened in the ruined church by the light of the moon.

The Laird challenged the sprightly tailor to make the trews by night in the haunted church. If the tailor could make these garments there for the Laird, the tailor would be handsomely rewarded.

The tailor, wanting the reward and thinking himself to be a sprightly fellow, agreed to the challenge. That night he set off to go and make the Lairds trews in the ruined church. He found a gravestone upon which to sit and lit candles all around him so he could see to sew the trews.

The tailor was well into sewing the garments without incident, thinking to himself that the Laird was going to have to pay when he won the challenge, when the ground shook. The tailor kept his fingers busy sewing as he looked around for the source of the disruption. From a stone in the ruined church, he saw a great head rise.

The head asked the tailor if he saw him, to which the tailor replied that indeed he did but he had a garment to sew so he could not stop stitching. The head rose a bit higher out of the ground until its neck was visible and again it asked the tailor if he now saw his neck.

The tailor replied that he did, but he still needed to keep stitching as he had a garment to finish. This continued as each time the other part of the spirit's body would rise a bit higher from the ground. Each time it would ask the tailor if he saw, and each time the tailor responded that he did, but he had to keep sewing.

The tailor continued to sew until the giant of a creature pulled out his first leg and stamped on the ground. The tailor knew he would have to hurry with the garment, so he took to doing a long stitch. By the time the creature had extracted his last leg the tailor was finished with his stitching, and took off out of the churchyard the newly made trews under his arm.

The giant raced after the tailor, hollering for him to stop, but the tailor did not. The tailor ran until he came upon the safety of Saddell castle, and shut the giant out. Angry, the giant took a swing, leaving his fingerprints embedded in the wall. But the tailor had won his bet, and the Laird paid him handsomely for his trews.

Each time the Laird wore his trews, he had the greatest tale to tell about a brave tailor who spotted the creature that lived beneath the stones at the ruined church. The tailor had not only lived to tell the tale, but had sewn the finest trews–though if the Laird had looked closer, he would have seen the long stitch.

Chapter 8: Celtic Mythical Creatures and Beasts

In the ages of myths and legends, there were reportedly all sorts of fantastic creatures and beasts running around, from mermaids to fairies, leprechauns, dragons, and magical horses. These creatures were either fierce and frightening, or simply magical beings. This chapter delves into some of these Celtic mythical creatures.

Black Dog (Faerie Hound)

Dogs, especially black dogs, have been considered as the guardians of the gates of hell throughout Europe for centuries. The Cu Sidhe, which means faerie hound, in Celtic myths are either green or black large dogs with glowing red eyes. Some of them are as big as a small horse.

They do the bidding of their fairy master, whether it is to abduct a human woman to nurse a fairy baby or guide a soul through the gates to the underworld. They say that this large dog is silent and can sneak up on a person more silently than a cat. Sometimes they will howl three times as they appear, and the sound can echo over a far distance. When men heard this sound they would lock up their womenfolk in fear of them being taken to the faerie realm. The black dog is a prominent figure in Scottish and Irish Celtic myths.

Bugul Noz

The Bugul Noz is a type of faerie creature found in Bretton that is so ugly that some say if you see him you will die. The Bugul Noz is not at all an evil creature; he is a kind and gentle soul, only he is so ugly that he hates for people to see him. He will try and frighten people or creatures away so they will not look at him. He even tries to keep the creature safe in the woods late at night, as this is the time he goes out. In the dark of the night, no one can see how hideous he is.

Dearg Due

Dearg Due never started out as a bloodsucking vampire; she was just a young woman of incredible beauty who wanted nothing more than to settle down with the man she loved. However, her father was a cruel and selfish man who thought of nothing but wealth and owning large amounts of land.

The young woman's father refused to let her marry her true love, a humble father, and instead sold her for wealth and land to their clan's chieftain. The chieftain was as cruel as any man could be, and treated her like she was a possession that he alone could see. He locked her up so no other could see her or go near her.

The young woman was so unhappy that she withered away to nothing and died. Her husband had already married another by the time they had buried her. Her true love was the only one who bothered to visit her grave and each day asked for her miraculous return.

On the eve of the first anniversary of her death, the young woman clawed her way from her grave, rage burning through her breast. Her one purpose for coming back to life on the eve was to seek revenge on those that had mistreated her so.

The first she called upon was her cruel and selfish father. While he slept, she placed her lips on his and sucked out his life force. Her next victim was her even crueler husband, whom she found in the middle of a group of lustful women. The woman ran out screaming when they saw her. She captured her husband, and instead of sucking the life out of him, she drank every drop of his life's blood.

The blood energized her and gave her great power; she felt stronger, faster, and had become immortal. From that day forward on the eve of the anniversary of her death, she arose, luring men in with her incredible beauty and feasting on their blood.

Groac'h

The Groac'h are water faeries of Bretton. They are known to be quite ugly and old; some have even been reported to have long walrus teeth. They mainly come out at night and can change their form; in some tales, they lure men in and turn them into fish. They then serve the fish up for dinner.

They have also been known to overwhelm humans with the gifts of their desires, and have the human beholden to them for the rest of their lives as a result. They live wherever there is water and can be found beneath the sand on the beach, caverns, and beneath the sea. Some of the Groac'h can control the forces of nature.

Morgens

Morgens are water sprites from Bretton mythology. They are a lot like sirens, whereby they sit upon the rocks brushing their hair seductively to lure sailors to their doom. There are quite a few stories about Morgens; there are a few variations of this mermaid type water-sprite. Just off the coast of Brittany, there are legendary little mermaid type people who are said to be quite beautiful to look upon. They kidnap people and take them to their crystal dwelling beneath the sea to be married. These little people are known as "morganezed" for the females, and "morganed" for the males.

In one story there was a beautiful human girl that was kidnapped by an old ugly morganezed; he took her to his dwelling at the bottom of the sea to become his bride. But his handsome son found her, and the two of them fell in love. The young morganezed rescued the young woman from his father and spirited her away.

Morvarc'h

Morvarc'h is a magical seahorse that has been known to be able to walk or gallop on the waves. It is a horse that pops up in quite a few Bretton legends, including the story of the Ys. The horse is said to be large with a shiny black coat and flowing mane. It can breathe fire and is fiercely loyal to its master.

Yan-gant-y-tan

Yan-gant-y-tan is a troll-like figure that roams the night and makes a nuisance of himself. The only way to tell him apart from other trolls is by the five candles he holds in his one hand, spinning them around. If you want him to leave you alone, you need to appease him with gold. He also does not like to turn around too fast, as he does not like to have his five candles go out.

Faeries

Celtic myths and legends are filled to the brim with tales of faeries. There are many different types of faeries, and they come in all shapes and sizes. Although each Celtic nation may have different names for each type of faery, they all share a few commonalities. A lot of the myths and legends do not paint faeries as very nice, as we are taught to think of them as young children. Some types of faeries can be quite malevolent; for example, some love to snatch human children and leave changelings in their place.

Leprechaun

The little green man with his hat, shamrock, and pot of gold is synonymous with the Irish. They believe they are lucky, while others believe they are a small nuisance that loves to play pranks and steal ale. They also like to make shoes for some reason, and every coin gold they find they store in a pot and hide it at the end of a rainbow. If a person is lucky enough to catch one, they are said to grant you three wishes if you let them go. But just like a genie, you have to be careful what you wish for, as everything has a price.

The leprechaun myth goes back for centuries and originates from the word "luchorpan," which translates to "little body." Luchorpan were water spirits that bonded with garden faeries to produce the leprechaun that developed a healthy taste for alcohol and would raid cellars.

Pooka

The Pooka, also spelled Puca, is a shapeshifting creature that likes to take the form of either a dog, a horse, a goblin, a rabbit, or goat. The earlier accounts of the pooka were always that of a pitch-black horse with a very long flowing mane and tail. The Pooka is known to have either gold or red glowing eyes.

Pooka can communicate with any creature they come in contact with; they love to twist a story. Small dark pools and bottomless lakes that look black are often called Pooka pools.

There are many interesting and varied stories about the pooka, but none where the creature actually harms or has any intent on harming anyone. They do love to chat with humans and have been known at times to give good advice.

Loch Ness Monster

The Loch Ness monster, or Nessy as she is referred to in modern times, was first sighted around 560 AD. Nessy came up out of the water and snatched a servant from the water's edge. In the age of monsters and dragons, the rumors of the monster in Loch Ness spread far and wide. After the first sighting, other strange happenings and sightings around Loch Ness have occurred which all refer to the giant sea monster or kelpie in Loch Ness.

Dragon

As with faeries, much folklore, myths, and legends have to include the huge fire-breathing dragons that once plagued the lands of Europe. There were all sorts of dragons and they took on various shapes, such as the large flying dragon with a huge wingspan and scaly body resembling a lion. Then there are the serpent shape dragons with long twisting bodies that look a bit like a snake with legs walking on tippy toes. There are many different types of dragons in all shapes and forms, even colors like the red dragon of Wales.

Some breathe fire, others breathe ice, they have tails like thick sharp arrows points at the end. Their tails are also usually powerful and their hands have talons that extend from their fingertips. They usually all have wings.

The Wulver of Shetland

The Wulver is a legend from the Shetland Islands and is a lot like the myth of the werewolf. The Wulver stands up like a human, complete with arms and legs. But instead of fingers or toes, it has claws. Its body is covered in hair and its head is that of a wolf. It has never been a human and it has never been a complete wolf. The Wulver is also not a shapeshifter; he stays in the form all the time.

The Wulver lives all alone in a cave on the Shetland Island, and lives in peace with the inhabitants there. He does not attack humans as long as they do not attack him. He is also not vicious or fearful, but instead has a kind and generous heart.

He loves to fish, and most have spotted him fishing off the rocks or around rocky pools. If he does come near humans it is to help those that have lost their way or are in danger. He has even been said to leave fish on the windowsill of those that are poor and hungry.

Kelpies

Kelpies are shape-shifting spirits that like to haunt the rivers and lakes in Scotland. Their preferred form is that of a horse. They like to pose as a docile beautiful pony standing grazing beside the edge of a lake or river, but that is just to lure people to them as they are malevolent spirits. They particularly love children; some say the one reason they take the shape of a pony is that most children are drawn to horses.

The thing about a Kelpie when they appear as a horse is that they encourage a person to climb upon their back or touch them. But they have a sticky hide, and once a person touches it, they are stuck to the Kelpie that will run into the nearest body of water and eat them.

Kelpies have also been known to appear in human form, as beautiful young women. Like the mermaids, they try to lure young men in so they can drown them. Some Kelpies like to take the form of a hairy, bone-crushing ogre-type creature that will lie in wait beneath the surface of the water. When someone gets near, they jump out and grab hold of the person, crushing them to death.

Another power a Kelpie has is that of summoning storms and flooding rivers. It is said that if you hear a loud wailing that is coming from a water's edge, it is a Kelpie warning of an imminent storm. The only way to catch a Kelpie is in its horse form as its bridle is its weak spot, but a caught Kelpie is very dangerous and has the strength of ten men.

Changelings

Changelings were said to be human babies that were swapped out by faeries or demons. The human babies are either given to the devil or taken to the fairy realm, where they would be used to strengthen the fairies' stock.

Many a deformed infant or imbecilic child would be thought to be a changeling. The only way to get rid of a changeling was to beat it, pinch it, or put a red hot poker on it. It was believed that abusing the changeling would send it back to where it came from, and the human baby would then be returned.

Naturally, this myth was responsible for a lot of child abuse during the times of the changeling belief. It was believed in olden times that infants were the most susceptible to demonic possession and easier to abduct by the fairies or demons.

Banshee

The Banshee is another type of faery in Irish mythology and legends. The Irish call her "scream caoine," which translates to keening, and her wail is believed to be the call of death. Those that hear her are being warned that there will soon be a death in the family.

It is believed that there is a Banshee for each family, and that they can be killed or deterred by a weapon made of pure gold. But even if she is killed, it will not stop the death of the family member. Legend says that even those who have tried to leave the area or country were never rid of the Banshee, as she would follow wherever they went.

The Blue Men of Minch

Not far off the coast of the Isle of Lewis lives a race of sea creatures. They are both male and female creatures that are much like mermaids and mermen. Their skin is said to be like the skin of a dolphin, and their legs resemble the dolphin's tail. They will use whatever wiles they can to lure sailors to a watery grave.

They live in caves along the craggy coastline between the Shiant islands and Pabail Uarach peninsular. They are thought to be the ancestors of Pasiphaê and Minos, who was the king of Crete. They were thought to have fled to the Mediterranean sea with the destruction of Crete and made their home in the Scottish Hebrides.

Finfolk

The Orkney islands sit off the north coast of Scotland in the cold, unforgiving North Sea. The Finfolk are creatures that would live deep beneath the waves of the North Sea during the winter months. The area in the North Sea where they live is called Finfolkaheem, and it can be found in the sea's deepest darkest depth.

During the winter months, the Finfolk do not cause much threat to humans, but when the summer months come they swim ashore and make Hildaland their home. They are cunning, shape-shifting monsters that abduct humans to take them to live in Finfolkaheem. Once there, they start to lose their human selves and gradually become the same as the Finfolk.

They come ashore during the summer months to find humans to abduct to keep their race alive. Finfolk were how some people, in those days, would explain mysterious happenings. They could also explain or justify the disappearance of people, especially the disappearance of young women.

Chapter 9: Celtic Bards, Druids, Holidays, and Festivals

The Celts believed in magic, gods, and wizards, and Druids held a high status in the tribe. Bards were also held in high regard, as they were the people who sang the Celts' history, triumphs, tragedies, and more.

The Bards of the Ancient Celts

Bards were the poets, musicians, and singers of the Celtic era. They would regale their audiences with the music and songs of great heroes, royalty, beasts, and so on. Bards were regarded as storytellers, to praise whoever employed them, and commemorate certain dates or victories.

There were not many kings who did not have a bard in their court to take note of the king's lineage, his stories, and triumph. They also employed them to sing of these accomplishments at great feasts.

Bards did not just get up one day and think, "I have a harp, so I am going to be a bard." They needed to be trained, and some even had apprenticeships with other bards before they could become one themselves.

Bards needed to be able to add to their songs and create ones practically on the fly without writing anything down. They were the custodians of the Celtic myths, legends, and folklore.

Taliesin, Chief of the Bards

Taliesin was the chief of the Bards and served in many of the kings throughout Britain. In the Arthurian legends, Taliesin served in the courts of King Arthur. He was as beautiful as he was talented, and he had the gift of prophecy to add to his lure.

Taliesin's name means "radiant bow," and was a Bard of great renown that charmed with his wit as well as his talent.

Mongán

There are many tales about Mongán, a bard and the son of the sea god, Manannan Mac Lir. Mongán's mother was Caíntigern, the Queen of Dál nAraide which made her the wife of King Fiachna Mac Báetáin. The kingdom over which Mongán's mother reigned was not a very nice kingdom. It was no surprise that the kingdom ran into problems for which they needed Manannan's help. Manannan said he would help, but only if Fiachna let him lay with his wife Caíntigern. With that union, Caíntigern fell pregnant with Mongán.

Manannan raised Mongán, and when he was a boy Mongán told his father that he had had a vision of his own death. He told his father that he would be killed with a stone his mother had picked up when they had gone for a walk together.

Caíntigern heard about this and was mortified that the beautiful stone she had taken from the beach would kill him. Caíntigern tried to throw the stone into the sea but the next day the stone was back on the sand.

Mongán eventually became the leader of the Dál nAraide and a poet.

Aengus

Aengus was the God of love and poetry, as well as the chief Bard to the Tuatha De Danann. Dagda was his father, so he inherited a few gifts for the great man. One of them was Dagda's love of music and poetry.

Aengus was charming, crafty, and could inspire the masses with his poetry. Unlike most other bards, Aengus had power over the dead and could resurrect them. He resurrected those he wished to with his power, which was the breath of life.

He was a young and beautiful man that could also shapeshift. His powers allowed him to woo both the young and the old.

The Druids of the Ancient Celts

The Druids are from the ancient Celts and were of a learned class. They practiced as advisors, teachers, judges, and priests to the Celtic people. Most of what is known about these mysterious people was told by Julius Caesar, and later by Christin Monks. Some scholars believe that a lot of what was recounted about the Druids was speculation. For Julius Caesar, the Celts were his sworn enemies and for the Christians, they were Pagans and heathens.

The Druids knew of the art of healing through various herbs, which they would brew up or use as a poultice. They were also known as the wise men of the village, and drawings usually depict them as cloaked older men. They would have long white beards, wear cloaks, and carry a long crook-type staff.

They were always called upon to be the judge of a dispute or any other type of accusation. There were usually some sort of tests if the Druid was unsure. The Druids would also be the ones to decree the punishment for any crimes committed or to settle arguments.

The chieftains and kings would rely upon the Druids for prophecy and to advise them. They were also in charge of the sacrifices and worship of the Celtic Gods. Within the sector of the Druids was also a hierarchy. One Druid was appointed the chief of Druids and would remain so until his death, when another would be appointed to the position.

Druids were never expected to join in any battle, rather they would stay away from the fight and ensure the Gods were appeased. This privilege drew a lot of people to want to join the order of the Druids. It was an honor to be accepted by the order, whereupon the student would be taught many studies such as astronomy, philosophy, verse, and about various herbs, potions, and healing arts.

Many feared the Druids as they had incredible power, not just mythical but within the Celtic societies. They had the power to get between warring nations and stop or prevent war. Through the supposedly prophetic visions and gifts of being able to see well into the future, kings and chieftains would turn to them for advice on many matters, including invasions and war.

There is a lot of speculation about the Druids' sacrificial practices. According to Julius Caesar, he believed that the Druids had no problem sacrificing prisoners of war or their own men to ensure that they were victorious over the enemies.

A lot of the megaliths that are found around ancient Celtic ruins, or where it was thought there was a Celtic burial or scarce ground, have megaliths associated with the Druids. These megaliths, such as the likes at Stonehenge, seem to be strategically placed to align with the stars, sun, and moon.

The Different Classes of the Druids

Within the Druid's sector, they had different classes of Druids and these reflected their standing or learned experience. The Druids class was represented by the color of the robes they wore:

- The Arch-druid, or Chief-druid, wore gold robes. He was also usually the eldest and most experienced Druid.
- The Druid below the Arch-druid wore white, and they acted as priests, judges, and mentors.
- The Druids who performed sacrifices wore red robes.
- The Druids who were the artists, scribes, and translators wore blue robes.
- The Druids who were learning wore black or brown robes.

Legendary Celtic Druids

There are quite a few legendary Celtic Druids of ancient times. A lot of wizards were thought of as Druids, in Irish legends, there were even female Druids.

Bodhmall

Bodhmall is a female Druid who appears in Irish legends in the Fenian Cycle. She was one of the caretakers of the famous Fionn mac Cumhaill (Finn MacCool) when he was a child.

Bodhmall was also a fierce warrior, and was one of the women charged with raising Fionn when he was sent away after his father was killed.

Merlin

Merlin is usually depicted as a powerful sorcerer or wizard. Merlin is based on a poet who was deemed a madman named Myrddin Wyllt, or in English Myrddin the Wild. He has appeared as Merlin throughout many Celtic myths and legends, including Arthurian. Merlin is probably one of the best known Druids of all the Celtic Druids.

Amergin Glúingel

In the Irish Mythological Cycle, Amergin was the Chief Ollam of Ireland. Amergin was a poet, bard, and a judge for the Milesian people. During the Milesians' conquest of Ireland and the battle of the three kings, Amergin acted as an impartial judge, laying down the laws of engagement.

Mug Ruith

Mug Ruith was a very powerful Druid on the Island that could change his size. He could grow as big as a giant, and his breath had the power to call up a storm or turn men to stone. He drove a chariot that at night would be as bright as the sun and was pulled by a band of oxen. It was believed that he could fly by means of a contraption called the Roth rámach, or oared wheel in English.

Tlachtga

Tlachtga was a powerful Druidess and the daughter of Mug Ruith. She had long fiery red hair and went everywhere with her father, learning his magical secrets and forging her own path. She gave birth to triplets upon a hill that was named for her called the Hill of Tlachtga in Ireland County Meath. Her triplets were said to be from different fathers after she was raped by three men. These three men were the sons of Simon Magus the sorcerer.

The Celtic Holidays, Festivals, and Celebrations

The Druids were a well ordered sect and were concerned with nature. Trees were sacred to them and they followed many of nature's patterns as their way of life. Their season cycle ran in line with the lunar and solar cycles, which is why they had eight main holy days of worship.

Samhain

Samhain was the ancient Celtic equivalent of the current New Year's Day. It fell on the 31st of October each year. It was a day for many celebrations because it was the day that the last of the harvesting would be done. It was also the day when the veil between the living and dead was said to be at its thinnest. This meant that the living and dead would be in close proximity to each other.

Yule

Yule was the celebration of the winter solstice. It was the night that the Druids would sit on sacred mounds for the entire night so they would be reborn again with the first rays on the sun.

Holly was associated with the long cold winter months, where people would hang it in their houses. It was a sign of hope and encouragement to push through the long dark days into the bright light of the summer.

Holly and mistletoe were sacred to the Druids, who were said to cut the trees six days before the winter solstice with a golden sickle. These two plants are still to this day a symbol of Christmas and winter in the Northern hemisphere.

Yule fell on the 21st of December, which was the longest night but the shortest day. For the Celts, winters were harsh and they did not have the luxury of central heating or goose down duvets. They tried to survive the long bitter winters as best they could. Yule marked the return of the sun to a frozen land so they would rejoice by gathering and having large bonfires.

The wine and ale flowed freely, while some of the livestock that had survived would be slaughtered, gathered, and rotated on large spits to feed the masses.

Imbolc

Imbolc is the holiday that marks the halfway point between winter and the coming spring. The celebration starts on the 1st of February and lasts until sundown on the 2 February. It usually follows the start of the animal breeding season, and is why the Celts celebrate the fertility Goddess Brigid on this day. It was a time of hope and the promise of the warmer spring days to come.

The celebration would be held by the Celts lighting a huge effigy of the Goddess which was made from bundles of rushes and oats. The Celts would have a huge celebration in the honor of the Goddess, and light various lamps and bonfires. By the end of the celebration, offerings of fruits, vegetables, and oats would be left.

Ostra

Ostra was the spring equinox and was celebrated on the day that the night and day are of equal length. This usually happens on or around the 20th of March and celebrates the Goddess Ostara. Ostra is a Goddess of fertility, and she's where the name "Easter" comes from. This was another day of celebrations where wine and ale would flow freely. Bonfires would be lit and feasts would be spread for all to enjoy.

Beltane

Beltane was the start of summer celebrations for the Celtic people. Beltane welcomed the change of seasons. The Celts did this with bonfires, feasts, and merriment to enjoy the warm bright weather of the season. This celebration usually took place on the 30th of April or 1 May.

Litha

There is a legend that during the winter and summer equinox the Holly King and the Oak go to war. At the time of the winter equinox, the Holly King wins and rules the dark cold days of the winter. During the summer equinox, the Oak King wins and rules the bright warm days of summer.

Litha is the summer solstice holiday and the day when the Celts would celebrate the Oak King's victory over the Holly King. It is also the longest day and shortest night that was celebrated on the 21 st of June.

Lughnasa

Lughnasa celebrated the first harvest of the year and took place in the autumn months on the 2nd of August. This day and holiday were associated with the God Lugh, to whom the Celtic people would offer the first pickings of their harvest in tribute.

Mabon

Mabon was the holiday that celebrated the autumn equinox and harvest moon. It was celebrated during the time in autumn when once again there was an equal time during the day and night. It was a celebration of balance, abundance, and sharing that took place on the 21 September.

Conclusion

Mythology can and has been depicted in many ways through the ages. All the interpretations we have today are from scripts or tales handed down from generations past. A lot of the scripts have been written in ancient languages that are also open for misinterpretation by the translator. Even the stories handed down from generation to generation would have been added to or told differently to what was told. Most everyone at some point in their life comes across the old game of broken telephone or Chinese whispers; the story whispered at the start of the telephone chain never comes out the same at the end of it. Handing down mythologies and legends is the same.

In our modern-day world, we are lucky enough to have scholars and advanced technology to help them dig a bit deeper into what we know as historical truths. It is thanks to these scholars, as well as the Celtic people keeping their heritage alive, that we get to become a part of their world. To have a better understanding of who we are, it is essential to know where we came from and the cultures that were our past. Learning about Celtic mythology, the folklore, fairy tales, druids, royalty, gods/goddesses, and all they entail keep these cultures alive for future generations.

In this book, we covered all the basic gods/goddesses, great legendary kings, and both fair and evil queens. We looked at some of the more popular fairy stories of the Celts and celebrated their most well-known heroes and heroines. You were introduced to bards and some of the most powerful druids, and learned about the Celtic culture, their mythical beasts, magic, festivals, and sacrifices. There is a lot more to Celtic mythology than presented here, as there is only so much a writer can squash into one book. But hopefully, this one book has inspired you to want to delve deeper into the adventure that is Celtic mythology. Even great writers like Shakespeare were inspired by the rich folklore of the Celts.

Many great books have been translated from the older texts that you can read and a host of information in various libraries on the subject. Of course, one of the best ways to find out more would be to take a trip to some of the heritage sites attributed to these myths and legends. These places always have vast treasure troves of information about their respective legends. It is when you visit these places that you realized just how diverse Celtic mythology truly is. The six nations that still hold a tribute to their Celtic heritages are Scotland, Ireland, Wales, Cornwall (Conaulles), the Isle of Man (Manx), and Brittany (North West Gual) in France. There are also parts of Galicia in Spain that still maintain parts of their Celtic heritage along with quite a few Celtic heritage sites.

Some good books having to do with Celtic mythology, folklore, and legends are:

- *Cath Maige Tuired*
- *The Cattle-raid of Cualnge (Tain Bo Cuailnge)*
- *Heroic Romances of Irelands (there are two volumes)*
- *Of Gods and Fighting Men*
- *The Books of the Takings of Ireland*
- *Cuchulain of Muirthemne*
- *VIII: The Battle of the Trees*
- *The Lament of the Old Woman of Bear*
- *Beira, Queen of Winter*
- *Part II Book IV: The Hunt of the Slieve Cuilinn*
- *Fairy and Folk Tales of the Irish Peasantry*
- *Fairy Legends and Traditions of the South of Ireland*

- *Pagan Celtic Britain: Studies in Iconography and Tradition*

We live in a world that through modern-day advances a lot of what most myths and legends were built on can be explained. However, there is still a lot that cannot be explained by science or technology. Even though the four corners of our world have been discovered, there are still many layers of it that have not. Strange and wondrous things are being discovered every day that makes us stop and go "Oh wow!" Maybe one day the things that were unexplained to us will go down as future generations' myths and legends.

I hope you enjoyed this journey through the romance, lure, battles, and wonders of all that is Celtic mythology as much as I enjoyed writing it for you. You should now have your own piece of the Celts' mysterious, ancient past to regale others with such as the bards once did. Unlike the bards, however, we have the power of the internet to help us spread their wonderfully creative and magical tales. Through books like this one and the interest of all its wonderful readers, these myths and legends will stay alive well into the future.

A SPIRITUAL START!

Start your week with gratitude, joy, inspiration, and love.

Healing, motivation, inspiration, challenge and guidance straight to your inbox every week!

FIND OUT MORE

References

Ankou. (n.d.). Wikipedia. https://en.wikipedia.org/wiki/Ankou

Ashliman, D. (2013). *Tristan and Isolde.* Pitt.edu. https://www.pitt.edu/~dash/tristan.html

Blue Men of Minch. (n.d.). Britain Explorer. https://britainexplorer.com/listing/blue-men-of-minch/

Breton Myths & Legends. (n.d.). Gites and More. http://www.gitesandmore.co.uk/Legends%20of%20%20Brittany.htm

Brittany. (n.d.). Britannica. https://www.britannica.com/place/Brittany-region-France

Bugul Noz. (n.d.). Wikipedia. https://en.wikipedia.org/wiki/Bugul_Noz

Celtic Mythology. (n.d.). Myths and Legends. http://www.mythencyclopedia.com/Ca-Cr/Celtic-Mythology.html

Changeling. (n.d.). Britannica. https://www.britannica.com/art/changeling-folklore

Classic Authors Writing About the Ancient Celts. (n.d.). People. https://people.stfx.ca/mlinklet/ClassicalAuthors.htm

Danu (Irish Goddess). (n.d.). Wikipedia. https://en.wikipedia.org/wiki/Danu_(Irish_goddess)

Fairy Bridge. (n.d.). Transceltic. https://www.transceltic.com/isle-of-man/fairy-bridge

Jacobs, J. (n.d.). *Jack and His Comrades*. Fairytalez. https://fairytalez.com/jack-comrades/

Johnson, B. (n.d.). The Kelpie. Historic UK. https://www.historic-uk.com/CultureUK/The-Kelpie/

Lady of The Lake. (2019, September 2). Encyclopedia.com. https://www.encyclopedia.com/literature-and-arts/literature-english/english-literature-1499/lady-lake

Lavandière de Nuit. (n.d.). A Book of Creatures. https://abookofcreatures.com/2015/04/17/lavandiere-de-nuit/

Lloyd, E. (2016, November 28). *Mythical Submerged City Of Ys – Europe's Own Sodom And Gomorrah*. Ancient Pages. http://www.anciehttpsntpages.com/2016/11/28/mythical-submerged-city-of-ys-europes-own-sodom-and-gomorrah/

MacQueen, D. (2018, March 24). *Finfolk, the sinister creatures of the deep and the hidden islands of Orkney*. Transceltic. https://www.transceltic.com/scottish/finfolk-sinister-creatures-of-deep-and-hidden-islands-of-orkney

MacQueen, D. (2018, April 20). *Wulver: Shetland's kind and generous werewolf*. Transceltic. https://www.transceltic.com/scottish/wulver-shetlands-kind-and-generous-werewolf

Merlin. (n.d.). Fandom. https://questforcamelot.fandom.com/wiki/Merlin

O'Regan, A. (2018, October 02). *The Dearg Due - How a revengeful young lover became Ireland's most famous female vampire.* https://www.irishcentral.com/culture/entertainment/dearg-dur

Owen, J. (2009, March 20). *Druids Committed Human Sacrifice, Cannibalism?.* National Geographic. https://www.nationalgeographic.com/news/2009/3/druids-sacrifice-cannibalism/#:~:text=Recent%20evidence%20that%20Druids%20possibly,of%20Druidic%20savagery%2C%20archaeologists%20say.

The Black Dog. Also known as Cu Sidhe or Coinn Iotair. (2011, June 14). Mayo Folk Tales. https://amayodruid.blogspot.com/2011/06/black-dog-also-known-as-cu-sidhe-or.html

The Three Crowns. (n.d.). Fairytalez. https://fairytalez.com/the-three-crowns/

Who Were Celts? (2019, October 24). History.com. https://www.history.com/topics/ancient-history/celts

Wright, G. (n.d.). *Celtic Gods.* Mythopedia. https://mythopedia.com/celtic-mythology/gods/